MW00509196

KETOGENIC DIET BEEF, SIDES AND SNACKS COOKBOOK

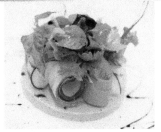

Felicity Flinn

Table of Contents

3

5

9

KETOGENIC DIET

LAMB AND BEEF COOKBOOK

LAMB

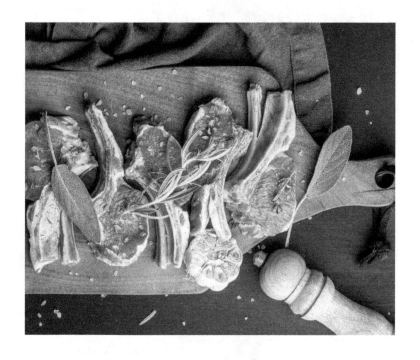

Roasted Oven Lamb Chops with Curry Sauce

(Ready in about 45 mins | Serving 4 | Difficulty: Medium)

Per serving: kcal: 251 Fat: 11g, Net Carbs: 8g, Protein: 27g

Ingredients

- 2 racks of lamb 2
- Melted ghee or olive oil 1 tsp
- Salt & pepper
- Garam masala 1-2 tsp

Indian curry sauce

- Ghee 1 tbsp
- Shallot- chopped 1
- Garlic cloves- chopped 3
- Ginger- chopped 1 tbsp
- Turmeric ½ tsp
- Fennel seed ½ tsp

- Mustard seed ½ tsp

- Diced tomatoes 1&1/2 c

- coconut milk (13 oz)

- salt 1 tsp

- Brown sugar or honey 1 tsp

- Garnish- cilantro, Aleppo chili flakes, toasted fennel seeds

Instructions

1. Preheat to 425F.

2. Cut off the extra fat and dry pat lamb. Rub with molten olive oil or ghee. Sprinkle the salt, black pepper & garam masala spice mixture on both sides (or use Indian curry powder) and put on a baking sheet & set aside.

3. Make a sauce. Heat ghee over low heat in a medium pot or wide sauté pan. Add shallot, ginger, and garlic, then mix for around 3-4 mins until golden. Add the turmeric, fennel seeds & mustard seeds as well as resume cooking, stirring for another minute.

4. Stir in sliced tomatoes & their juices. Continue to cook & mix for another 5 minutes before the tomato split some down. Add in coconut milk, leaves of fenugreek, salt & sugar.

5. Stir in, test, adjust salt.

6. Bring to a boil, reduce heat to medium, & let it simmer while the lamb is being baked.

7. Put the lamb in a hot oven, roast for 10 mins, flip over, cook for another ten mins, then flip over again & broil for a few minutes if you want a crispy crust. Beware about not burning when broiling.

8. Take the lamb out of the oven. Let rest for 5-10 mins, then slice over & plate or platter over fenugreek sauce.

9. Sprinkle with (optional) fresh cilantro, toasted fennel seeds & chili flakes (Aleppo chili is nice), if you prefer.

10. Notes: Vegetarians should also serve the delicious sauce over roasted vegetables or baked tofu.

Grilled Charmoula Lamb Chops

(Ready in about around 70 mins | Serving 4 | Difficulty: Medium)

Per serving: kcal: 519, Fat: 43g, Net Carbs: 1.5g, Protein: 31g

Ingredients

- Lamb loin chops 8
- Olive oil 1 tsp
- Ras el Hanout 2 tbsp
- Salt>>to taste

For the Charmoula

- Fresh chopped mint 2 tbsp
- Fresh chopped parsley ¼ c
- Lemon zest 2 tbsp
- Chopped garlic cloves 3

- Smoked paprika ½ tsp
- Red pepper flakes 1 tsp
- Olive oil ¼ c
- Lemon juice 2 tbsp
- Salt & pepper >>to taste

Instructions

1. Using olive oil to cook the lamb and generously cover with salt. Generously season with salt, pepper & a little cumin.) Preheat your grill and grill for around 2 minutes a side for a medium-rare. Let the meat take a few minutes to rest before eating.

For the chermoula

1. Combine all the Charmoula components in a food processor or magic bullet & pulse up to a consistency close to pesto. Don't over blend-it shouldn't be liquified completely.
2. With helpful support from Charmoula & some new lemon zest, serve the lamb chops. Perfect with

grilled asparagus and cauliflower puree on the side.

Garlic & Herb Crusted Lamb Chop

(Ready in about 6-8 hrs.| Serving 4 | Difficulty: Medium)

Ingredients

- lamb rib chops 2 lbs.

- garlic cloves pressed 5

- olive oil 4 tbsp

- fresh parsley plus more for garnish 2 tbsp

- Tabasco original red pepper sauce 2 tsp

- salt 1 tsp

- black pepper freshly ground 1 tsp

- dried thyme ¼ tsp

For the Sauce:

- chicken or beef stock ½ c

- unsalted butter softened 2 tbsp

Instructions

How to Make Lamb Chops with Garlic Butter Sauce:

1. With paper towels, carefully pat lamb chops off, brushing away any potential bone bits or flakes. Cut between ribs to divide cuts, chopping small parts into 3/4 "or 1" wide.

2. In a measuring cup, add the marinade ingredients: Five pressed garlic cloves, 3 tbsp of olive oil, 2 tbsp of parsley, 2 tsp of Tabasco, 1 tsp of cinnamon, 1 tsp of pepper, and 1/4 tsp of thyme.

3. Put lamb chops in a non-metal casserole bowl, sprinkle over marinade, and rub both sides of lamb chops with marinade (focusing on meaty portions). Refrigerate & cover for 6 to 18 hours.

4. Let the lamb chops stay at room temp 30 min before cooking. Heat large, heavy pan over high

heat. Add 1 tbsp of oil to the hot pan &, once the oil is heated, apply the lamb chops & sear 3-4 minutes per side depending on the thickness of the chops and the required doneness. Bear in mind that the temperature increases by 5 degrees while it rests (see notes). The lamb will be average doneness at 3 minutes per side, and the lamb will be fair-good to fully finish at 4 min per side. If your pan is not big enough to accommodate all lambs' chops, sear in two separate pans.

To make the pan sauce,

1. Remove extra oil from the pan (leave in 1 to 2 Tablespoons oil) & be cautious not to drain the flavorings and drippings.
2. Add 1/2 cup stock & boil for 2 minutes. Then switching off heat & mix in 2 tbsp of soft butter, 1 tbsp at a time. Spoon sauce on top of lamb chops and, if desired, garnish with more parsley.

Keto Paleo Pesto Sauce with Lamb Chops

(Ready in about 40 mins | Serving 4 | Difficulty: Medium)

Per serving: kcal: 603, Fat: 51.6g, Net Carbs: 1.9g, Protein: 34.9g

Ingredients:

- Rack of Lamb 1
- Sea salt >> to taste
- Pepper >> to taste
- Ghee 2 tbsp
- Basil leaves 4 c
- Pine nuts or walnuts ½ c
- Olive oil ½ c
- Lemon, juiced 1

Instructions:

1. Heat the oven to 350 ° C.
2. Place a healthy skillet on an oven over medium to high heat & melt the ghee. Sprinkle with enough salt & pepper over the lamb.
3. Place the lamb down on one side while the skillet is hot to sear it for 1 minute when pressing gently. Then spin around until it sears both edges.
4. Put the skillet in the oven with the lamb & bake for medium or more for well-cooked for 7-10 minutes.
5. Remove from the oven and put it to rest on a cutting board.
6. The salt & pepper, fresh basil, pine nuts, olive oil, & lemon are put in the food processor while the lamb rest.
7. Pulse the mixture until smooth &, if necessary, apply a little more grease, then scrape the sides down until well mixed.
8. Cut the lamb onto the bones and put the chops on the dishes.
9. Serve & eat. Top with pesto.

Easy Pan-Seared Mustard Cream Sauce Lamb Chops

(Ready in about 30 mins | Serving 4 | Difficulty: Easy)

Per serving: Kcal: 426, Fat: 30g, Net Carbs: 4g, Protein: 31g

Ingredients

Pan-Seared Lamb Chops

- 1 & 1/2 lb. lamb chops, 6 chops
- Garlic cloves minced 2
- Minced rosemary 1 tbsp
- Olive oil 2 tbsp
- Salt & pepper>> to taste

Mustard Cream Pan Sauce

- Minced shallot 1 tbsp
- beef broth ½ c
- Brandy 2 tbsp
- Heavy cream 2/3 c
- grainy mustard like Maille 1 tbsp
- 2 teaspoons lemon juice 2 tsp
- 2 teaspoons Worcestershire sauce 2 tsp
- 1 teaspoon erythritol 1 tsp
- Butter 2 tbsp
- the sprig of rosemary and sprig of thyme
- salt & pepper>> to taste

Instructions

1. Lamb Chop Prep: The day before-In a small bowl with 1 tbsp of olive oil, put the minced rosemary & garlic. Trim off any extra fat (or leftover bones) from the lamb chops, leaving around 1/8 of an

inch of the thin layer of fat. Place the lamb chops in a shallow baking dish on a single sheet, & season with salt & pepper on both sides. Smooth all sides of each lamb chop with the garlic-rosemary-oil. Cover with plastic tape, then overnight refrigerate.

2. Prep: Day of-Carry the lamb thirty minutes at room temp. Mince the shallot & lemon juice. Keep the rosemary & thyme sprigs ready for use. Place the other ingredients next to the pot or weigh them and wait.

3. Cooking: Fire up a large (non-stick or stainless) frying pan over medium heat. Apply 1 tbsp of oil when heated, stirring to cover the saucepan. In one plate, add the lamb chops & transform heat down to normal. Let the lamb chops cook for 6-7 mins uninterrupted. Switch on and cook for another 6-7 mins, depending on how fresh your lamb chops are. Lift the lamb onto a platter & cover with foil loosely.

4. Mustard Cream Pan Sauce: Reduce the heat to medium-low, then add the shallots & sauté until

softened. Attach the beef broth & brandy and return the heat to normal. Simmer & apply the mustard, Worcestershire sauce & erythritol for 1 minute. To mix, swirl or whisk.

5. Whisk in the cream, then add the rosemary sprig & thyme. Let it cool for 7- 8 mins or until almost your perfect consistency- it'll thicken as it cools. Add the butter & lemon juice, then blend. Simmer until the sauce becomes deep and shiny. Check the seasoning.

6. Remove the rosemary & thyme sprigs until the lamb chops are being sauced & cooked.

Paleo Dairy-Free Tzatziki Lamb Burgers

(Ready in about 20 mins | Serving 4 | Difficulty: Easy)

Per serving: kcal: 505, Fat: 44g, Net Carbs: 1g, Protein: 25g

Ingredients

For the Burgers:

- 1 lb. Grass-fed ground lamb 1 lb.

- 1/4 cup chopped green onions scallions or red onion ¼ c

- 1 tbsp chopped fresh dill 1 tbsp

- 1/2 tsp dried oregano ½ tsp

- 1 tbsp fresh mint finely chopped 1 tbsp

- Pinch of crushed red pepper

- Fine-grain sea salt>> to taste

- 1 tbsp water 1 tbsp

- olive oil to grease pan 1 tsp

For the Tzatziki

- Garlic cloves 3

- 1 can full-fat coconut milk chilled, and all but 1 tbsp of the liquid part discarded

- cucumber, chopped 1 med

- fresh-squeezed lemon juice 2.5 tbsp

- chopped fresh dill 2 tbsp

- sea salt >> to taste

- Black pepper >> to taste

Instructions

1. I suggest making Tzatziki at least 2 hours before serving to encourage the blending of the coconut cream's flavors and thickening. You can even

create it the day before, then place it in the fridge tightly sealed.

Make the Tzatziki:

1. In a high-speed blender or food processor, place the garlic, cucumber, and lemon juice and pulse until finely chopped. Drop milk, dill, cinnamon, and pepper into the coconut and combine until blended. The sauce isn't going to be smooth.
2. Once mixed, taste whether to add salt or pepper. Switch to a lidded box & keep in the refrigerator until serving time. Over time, the aromas can increase as it chills in the freezer.

For the Burgers:

1. Gently combine the ground lamb in a mixing bowl with the scallions OR red onion, dills, oregano, mint, red pepper & water. Sprinkle the mixture with salt from the sea of fine grain, then shape into 4 patties of a similar amount. Don't overwork the beef-only manage sufficiently to shape the patties.

2. Heat a broad cast-iron skillet over med-hi heat and apply a tiny amount of olive oil to clean. Sprinkle with the fine grain of sea salt gently on the skillet.

3. Put the patties in the skillet & cook for around 4 minutes on either side-change the heat needed to avoid too much browning on the exterior. You should barbecue or broil the burgers as an option.

4. Take off the skillet and serve over vegetables, Greek salad, and finish with tzatziki sauce. If desired, you may also serve it on the side for dipping. Garnish with fresher spices if you prefer-enjoy them.

Keto Lamb Meatballs & Mint Gremolata

(Ready in about around 20 mins | Serving 24 meatballs | Difficulty: Medium)

Per serving: kcal: 306, Fat: 17g, Net Carbs: 2g, Protein: 35g

Ingredients

For the meatballs:

- Ground lamb 2lbs.
- Eggs 2
- Superfine Almond flour ½ c
- Fresh chopped parsley ¼ c
- Minced garlic clove 1
- Za'atar seasoning 1&1/2 tbsp
- Kosher salt 1 tsp
- Water3 tbsp
- Olive oil for frying 2 tbsp

For the gremolata:

- Chopped fresh parsley 2 tbsp

- Chopped fresh mint 2 tbsp

- Lime zest 1 tbsp

- Minced garlic cloves 2

Instructions

For the meatballs

1. Combine the meatball components in a medium bowl (except olive oil), and blend well.
2. Shape into 24 one & a half inches (approximately) of meatballs.
3. Heat olive oil over medium heat in a non-stick sauté pan.
4. Cook the meatballs on both sides in batches before they brown & cook through – between 2-3 minutes per side.
5. Remove the cooked meatballs & put them on a lined sheet of paper towel before ready to serve.
6. Serve warm, sprinkled with a gremolata.

For the gremolata:

1. In a shallow bowl, add the ingredients & stir well.

Keto Lamb Roasted with Chimichurri Sauce

(Ready in about 4 hrs | Serving 10 | Difficulty: Medium)

Per serving: kcal: 537, Fat: 46g, Net Carbs: 1g, Protein: 32g

Ingredients

- Chopped fresh rosemary 2 tbsp
- Garlic powder 1&1/2 tbsp
- Sea salt & ground pepper
- Unsalted melted butter 3 tbsp
- Boneless trimmed & tied lamb shoulder roast 4 lb.
- Chimichurri Sauce

Instructions

1. Mix the rosemary, garlic powder, One tablespoon salt, and 1 tsp pepper in a small container. Add butter to create a paste, then blend. Brush the

lamb deeply with the paste of garlic-herb, then rub it with your hands to cover fully with the meat. In a zip-lock bag, put the roast & chill for two hours or overnight.

2. Oven temperature to 375 ° F (230 ° C). Place the lamb on a rack in a roasting pan & roast until the thermometer reads 130 ° F (55 ° C) for rare or 140 ° F (60 ° C) for medium-rare, 1 3/4 to 2 hours, tenting the lamb with foil for the last cooking hour to prevent it from being too brown. Enable meat to rest 20 minutes (or 45 minutes) before slicing.

3. Slice small & eat with a side chimichurri sauce.

Instant Pot Lamb Curry – Keto

(Ready in about 35 mins | Serving 4 | Difficulty: Easy)

Per serving: Kcal: 275, Fat: 10g, Net Carbs: 13g, Protein: 29g

Ingredients

- Lamb stew meat 500 g
- Butter 1 tbsp
- Diced onion 1
- Minced garlic cloves 2
- Fresh ginger minced 2 tbsp
- Ground cardamom 1 tsp
- Cloves whole 3
- Ground coriander 2 tsp
- Turmeric 1 tsp
- Garam masala 1 tbsp

- Cumin 2 tsp
- Salt 1 tsp
- diced tomatoes with juice 400g can
- Kale chopped 2 c
- Zucchini chopped 1
- Bell pepper chopped 1

Instructions

1. Melt butter into sauté mode at the bottom of the Instant Pot container.

2. Then add the onions, garlic, ginger & lamb when the butter is melted. Give it a simple swirl and introduce the remaining ingredients with the addition of kale, zucchini, and pepper bell. Mix well.

3. Cover the lid & turn the pressure lever to seal. Use the "manual," "pressure cook," "or" meat/stew "button to cook the curry for 20 minutes at high pressure. Enable the pressure to escape automatically for at least 7-10 minutes before manually removing the strain. It is recommended

to escape a natural strain, although not mandatory for the doneness.

4. Switch the Instant Pot back to sauté mode & add the kale, zucchini & bell peppers. Enable the curry to cook for around five minutes or until the vegetables are soft. Switch off the Instant Pot and eat. Garnish with fresh coriander or cilantro.

Rosemary Dijon Lamb Chops Roasted

(Ready in about 15 mins | Serving 4 | Difficulty: Medium)

Per serving: Kcal: 446, Fat: 40g, Net Carbs: 2g, Protein: 18g

Ingredients

- Dijon mustard 1 tbsp
- Minced garlic cloves 2
- Olive oil 3 tbsp
- Chopped fresh rosemary 2 tsp
- Salt ½ tsp
- Pepper ¼ tsp
- Lamb loin chops with bone-in 2 lb.

Instructions

1. In a container, whisk together Dijon mustard, garlic, olive oil, rosemary, salt & pepper. Put lamb chops or other airtight containers in a large zip-top

case. Cover lamb on both ends, with Dijon combination. Let marinate in the refrigerator for a minimum of 30 minutes to up to 24 hours.

2. Place an oven rack in the oven's highest spot and line a broiler pan with aluminum foil.

3. Take off the bag lamb chops & put them on the prepared plate. Place oven on top to broil and pan into the oven.

4. Cook lamb chops for 8 mins, until crispy, then turn over and cook for an extra 3-5 minutes depending on the meat's doneness. (3 minutes on extremely unusual, 4 minutes on average, 5 minutes on well done)

Keto Lamb Fajitas

(Ready in about 60 mins | Serving 8 | Difficulty: Medium)

Per serving: kcal: 617, Fat: 42g, Carbs: 14g, Protein: 45g

Ingredients

- Lamb chunks 2 lb.

- Sliced red bell pepper 1

- Sliced yellow bell pepper 1

- Sliced green bell pepper 1

- Small white onion 1

- Diced green chili peppers 4 oz can

- Diced jalapenos 4 oz can

- Cauliflower rice 3 cups

- Gluten-free taco seasoning 2 packs

- Olive oil 4 tbsp

- Cumin 1 tsp

- Cinnamon 1/4

- Salt & pepper>> to taste

- Avocado & salsa

Instructions

1. Heat 2 tablespoons of olive oil over the moderate flame in a medium-sized pan. Add peppers, cumin, onion, & cinnamon. Then add salt & pepper to taste if desired. Mix well enough and sauté (about 20 minutes) until tender.

2. Meanwhile, heat 2 tablespoons of olive over medium heat in a separate pan. To taste, add chunks of lamb and salt & pepper. Sauté (about 10 minutes) until completely done. Drain excess liquid when done, then add taco seasoning & stir well.

3. Add cauliflower rice, chili peppers, and jalapenos to a third pot. Warm for about five minutes.

4. Serve in bowls such as avocado & salsa with optional toppings.

Keto Paleo Lamb Korma

(Ready in about 1hr. 10 mins | Serving 4 | Difficulty: Medium)

Per serving: Kcal: 383, Fat: 26.8g, Carbs: 11g, Protein: 29g

Ingredients

- Lamb stew meat 1 &1/2 lb.
- Coconut oil 2 tbsp
- Diced large shallots 2
- Quartered bottom mushrooms 10 oz
- Korma paste 6 tbsp
- Full fat coconut milk, 1 can
- Baby spinach 50 oz
- Juice of 1 lemon

- Unsweetened coconut yogurt or Greek yogurt 2-3 tbsp

Homemade korma paste:

- Garlic cloves 4

- Thumb-sized fresh ginger 2 piece

- Cayenne pepper ½ tsp

- Garam masala powder 2 tsp

- Sea salt 1&1/2 tsp

- Tomato puree or diced tomato without sugar 2 tbsp

- Fresh small green chilies 2

- Shredded coconut 4 tbsp

- Almond flour 3 tbsp

- Fresh cilantro 1 small bunch

- Cumin seeds 4 tsp

- Coriander seeds 2 tsp

- Coconut oil 3 tbsp

Instructions

To Make Homemade Korma Paste:

1. Grind cumin + seeds of coriander or use a pestle & mortar until it is perfect.
2. About chop/slice garlic, ginger, green chilies, and coriander.
3. Heat a frying pan with 3 tbsp of coconut oil over medium-high heat, then add ingredients from steps 1 and 2 when heated. Toast them gently until they are fragrant. Be alert not to let the spices fire.
4. Pour them into a food processor, grind them until the paste is smooth.
5. Put aside to freshen up. (We can use 6 tbsp of korma paste for 1 1/2 lb. of lamb meat. Store the excess paste for potential usage in a freezer.

To make Lamb Korma Curry:

1. Heat 2 tbsp of coconut oil over medium-high heat in a wide saucepan or deep frying pan, then add shallots when heated. Stir-fry gently when cooled.

2. Switch the fire to the extreme and apply sliced meat to the lamb. Pan fry for 4-5 mins, until browned gently.

3. Add coconut milk & 6 tbsp of korma paste. Connect the ingredients and fry for another min. Cover & put to simmer with a top.

4. Reduce heat to medium-low or low after boiling. Simmer until the lamb is ready, for 35-40 minutes. (Add a few tablespoons of water or chicken/vegetable supply if the sauce is too dry).

5. Add the spinach and mushrooms & turn over the fire for another minute.

6. Stir in lime juice & coconut milk before eating to marble the sauce.

Lamb Curry with Spinach

(Ready in about 4 hrs. 10 mins | Serving 4 | Difficulty: Medium)

Per serving: kcal: 158, Fat: 6.3g, Net Carbs: 3.9g, Protein: 20.3g

Ingredients

- Red onion sliced 1
- Garlic cloves 2
- Ginger crushed 2 tbsp
- Ground cardamom 2 tsp
- Whole cloves 6
- Coriander ground 2 tsp
- Turmeric powder 1 tsp
- Chili powder ½ tsp
- Garam masala powder 1 tsp
- Cumin powder 2 tsp
- Cubed lamb 500 g

- Packet frozen spinach 500 g
- Canned tomatoes chopped 400 g

Instructions

1. Defrost the freezer spinach, then push the handfuls to bring the excess water out (don't press too tightly to leave it dry).
2. In the slow cooker, place both ingredients, whisk.
3. Cook 4-5 hours on Heavy, or 8 hours on Average.

Lamb Curry Home-Style

(Ready in about 1 hr. 50 mins | Serving 4 | Difficulty: Easy)

Per serving: Kcal: 470, Fat: 29g, Carbs: 11g, Protein: 39g

Ingredients

- Thumb-sized ginger, ½ piece
- Quartered onions 2
- Garlic cloves 4
- Rapeseed oil 2 tbsp
- Cinnamon stick 1
- Ground coriander 1 tbsp
- Ground cumin 1 tsp
- Ground turmeric 1 tsp
- Fennel seeds ½ tsp
- Diced leg of lamb 750 g

- Chopped tomatoes 400g can

- Sliced & deseeded red chili or green chili 1

- Chopped small bunch of coriander

- Basmati rice & raita, to serve

Instructions:

1. Put ½ of ginger's thumb-sized slice, Two quartered onions & Four garlic cloves into a 300ml water food processor. Smooth purée with the blast.

2. Rub the sides down with a spoon & blitz again to get it as clean as possible. Top into a large sauté plate, cover for 15 minutes with a lid & simmer.

3. Remove the cover and proceed to cook for 5 minutes, stirring regularly. Much of the liquid should be gone by now. If not, then simmer for a little longer.

4. Apply 2 tbsp of rapeseed oil & the remaining slice of ginger to the saucepan, sliced into matchsticks. Switch the heat up and cook, stirring, until it begins to color for 3-5 minutes.

5. Stir in 1 cinnamon leaf, 1 tbsp of coriander powder, 1 tsp of cumin powder, 1 tsp of turmeric ground, and 1⁄2 tsp of fennel seeds, then apply 750 g of lamb neck. Stir-fry until color changes on the lamb.

6. Cut tomatoes in 400 g with a can of water, and 1 preferred & sliced red or green chili, season well, cover, and cook for 1 hour.

7. Extract from a tiny bunch of coriander the finely chopped stalks, re-cover and roast for the remaining 30 minutes until the lamb is tender. If required, apply a splash of water to break the consistency as it cooks.

8. Whisk in the finely cut coriander leaves & serve with chutney or raita basmati rice and mango.

BEEF

Keto Low-Carb Lasagna Stuffed Peppers

(Ready in about 60 mins | Serving 6 | Difficulty: Medium)

Per serving: kcal: 412, Fat: 27g, Net Carbs: 8g, Protein: 30g

Ingredients

- large Bell pepper 6

- Ground beef 1&1/2 lb.

- minced Garlic cloves 4

- Marinara sauce 2 c

- Italian seasoning 1 tbsp

- Ricotta cheese 1 c

- Mozzarella cheese 1 c

- Sea salt >>to taste

- Black pepper>>to taste

Instructions

1. Heat a skillet over medium-high heat to cook the meat sauce. Attach the garlic, and cook until fragrant, for around 30 seconds. Stir in the ground beef. Cook until browned, splitting apart the meat with either a spoon or spatula (about 10 minutes).

2. Stir in Italian seasoning and marinara sauce. Garnish with pepper and salt. Lower the heat to a medium simmer. Preheat the oven and cook the peppers, boil for about ten minutes.

3. Preheat the oven until 375 °F (191 ° C). Top a foil-coated baking tray or silicone pad.

4. Chop off the tops to cook the peppers, then scrape out the inner seeds then ribs. Cut a small layer off bottoms (without leaving a hole if possible) to allow the peppers to stand erect and secure.

5. Layer 1-2 tbsp (15-30 mL) each of ricotta cheese, meat sauce, and sliced mozzarella cheese within the bell peppers to mount the lasagna cups. (You'll like a bit more meat sauce than the other 2 layers.)

Repeat before the peppers are packed to the full, with the top sheet of mozzarella.

6. Place the peppers with aluminum foil on a lined baking tray and cover to guarantee that the foil does not contact the cheese. Bake thirty minutes. Remove the foil & bake for another 10 minutes before the cheese melts and browns.

Keto Baked Pepperoni Chips

(Ready in about 6 mins | Serving 6 | Difficulty: Easy)

Per serving: kcal: 116, Fat: 10g, Protein: 5g

Ingredients

- Pepperoni slices 5 oz

Instructions

1. To 400 °F, preheat the oven. Place an oven-safe rack over a wide sheet of baking.
2. Arrange slices of pepperoni over the plate.
3. Bake until crispy, for around 5-7 minutes. Cool for the crisp.

Thai Spicy Beef Salad

(Ready in about 16 mins | Serving 4 | Difficulty: Easy)

Per serving: kcal: 426, Fat: 26g, Net Carbs: 7g, Protein: 38g

Ingredients

Steak:

- Flank steak 1.5 lb.

- Sea salt 1 tsp

- Olive oil 1 tbsp

Salad:

- Chopped Bibb lettuce 6 c

- Chopped Cucumbers 1 c

- Grape tomatoes 1 c

- Fresh chopped cilantro ¼ c

- Basil ¼ c

- Sliced Red onion ¼ c

Dressing/marinade:

- Coconut aminos ¼ c

- Olive oil ¼ c

- Lime juice 2 tbsp

- Fish sauce 1 tbsp

- Thai red curry paste, 1 tbsp

- Black pepper ¼ tsp

Instructions

1. Whisk the dressing/marinade mixture together in a tiny bowl-coconut aminos, olive oil, lemon juice, sauce of fish, Thai red curry paste & black pepper, if necessary. If you need more spice, apply additional curry paste or pepper to taste,

2. The steak is properly flavored with sea salt on both sides. Put the steak in a single sheet in an 8x8 inch crystal baking tray or a Ziplock container. Pour 1/2

of the marinade on the steak (reserve the remaining for dressing).

3. Cover with plastic wrap over the meat & refrigerate for 2 - 8 hours. (If you do so any longer, the meat will get mush.) Cover the reserved sauce and refrigerate.

4. Merge all the salad ingredients in a large container, right before the meat is marinated.

5. Heat the beef in a grill pan accompanied by the oven-use this method to heat steak in the oven but only use olive oil rather than butter.

6. After cooking, allow the beef to rest for 5 minutes, then slice rather very thinly against the grain.

7. Serve the salad on top of grilled meat and dressing on the side.

Greek Baked Stuffed Tomato

(Ready in about 1 hr. 25 mins | Serving 4 | Difficulty: Medium)

Per serving: kcal: 499, Fat: 36g, Net Carbs: 7g, Protein: 34g

Ingredients

- Large Tomatoes 8

- Olive oil 3 tbsp

- Balsamic vinegar 1 tbsp

- Italian seasoning 2 tsp

- Sea salt 1&1/2 tsp

- Diced large Onion ½

- minced Garlic cloves 2

- Ground beef 1 lb.

- Black pepper ¼ tsp

- Cauliflower rice 12 oz

Instructions

1. To 375 °F preheat the oven. Cover a baking plate, or oil it.

2. Slice the tomatoes over the tops. Chop down the flesh and pass it to a big blender. Pick off as much flesh as feasible without puncturing outside skin.

3. Place the tomatoes on top or beside them, cut side up, on to baking platter with "lids." Place on the side.

4. To the blender, transfer Italian seasoning, balsamic vinegar, 2 tbsp (30 mL) of olive oil, and 1/2 teaspoon of sea salt. Mix until smooth. Place on aside.

5. Heat the remaining One tbsp cubic (15 mL) olive oil over medium heat in a big sauté pan. Add the sliced onions & saute until browned for almost ten minutes.

6. Add the sliced garlic, saute for around a min, until it is fragrant.

7. Stir in the ground beef. Season with pepper and sea salt. Increases temp to moderate-high. Cook for about ten minutes when browned & cooked through, splitting apart by a spatula.

8. Add the mixture of cauliflower rice & tomato pulp as well as the liquid. It is going to be warm, much like broth. Increase pressure to boil and cook. Simmer, stirring regularly, for about ten minutes, before the liquid diminishes, and you wind up in tomato sauce with beef & cauliflower rice. The cauliflower rice should be tender. Sea salt & pepper adjust to taste.

9. Pat with paper towels on the inner side of the tomatoes to get rid of excess moisture. In the baking dish, stuff the beef/cauliflower mixture onto the hollow tomatoes. Put "lids" on top of the tomato.

10. Cover with foil over the packed tomatoes & bake for thirty mins. Uncover & bake for another 15-20 mins, until the tomatoes are tender & pucked on the corners.

Keto Low-Carb Crack Slaw Egg Rolls in a Bowl

(Ready in about 15 mins | Serving 4 | Difficulty: Easy)

Per serving: kcal: 455, Fat: 31.6g, Net Carbs: 7.5g, Protein: 33.3g

Ingredients

- Avocado oil 1 tbsp

- Minced Garlic cloves 4

- Fresh ginger 3 tbsp

- Ground beef 1 lb.

- Sea salt 1 tsp

- Black pepper ¼ tsp

- Shredded coleslaw mix, 4 c

- Coconut aminos ¼ c

- Toasted sesame oil 2 tsp

- Green onions ¼ c

Instructions

1. Heat the avocado oil over medium to high heat in a big saute pan. Add ginger & garlic. Sauté for approximately one minute, before fragrant.
2. Add the ground meat. Season with pepper & sea salt. Cook for around 7-10 mins, until browned.
3. Reduce to moderate heat. Add coconut aminos & coleslaw mixture. Stir for covering. Cover & cook until the cabbage is ready, for around five minutes.
4. Remove from flame. Add the toasted salami oil & green onions.

Keto Korean Beef Bowl

(Ready in about 20 mins | Serving 4 | Difficulty: Easy)

Per serving: kcal: 513, Fat: 36g, Net Carbs: 9g, Protein: 35g

Ingredients

Cauliflower rice:

- Olive oil 1 tbsp

- Cauliflower 1 lb.

- Sea salt ½ tsp

- Black pepper 1/8 tsp

Beef:

- Olive oil 1 tbsp

- Ground beef 1 lb.

- Sea salt ½ tsp

- Minced Garlic cloves 4

- Coconut aminos ¼ c

- Beef broth ¼ c

- Sesame oil 2 tsp

- Ground ginger ¼ tsp

- Crushed red pepper flakes ¼ tsp

Garnish:

- Sliced Green onions ¼ c

- Sesame seeds 1 tsp

- Sliced small Cucumber 1

Instructions

1. In a wide wok, heat 1 tbsp (15 mL) of olive oil over moderate to high flame. Transfer cauliflower rice in the wok. Where needed, season with salt & black pepper. Sauté for about 3-5 mins, when fully done.

2. Remove from flame, set aside, & cover the cauliflower rice to stay warm.

3. Whisk the coconut aminos, broth of beef, ground ginger, sesame oil, & chili flakes together in a tiny cup. Place aside the sauce.

4. Adjust heat to medium-high. Add one more spoonful of olive oil (15 mL) into the wok. Add the minced beef & salt for seasoning. Cook for around 8-10 mins, split via spatula & periodically mix, until browned.

5. Get well in the beef & add the chopped garlic. Sauté for around a minute, then add in the meat, until it is fragrant.

6. Pour over the beef sauce. Carry to a boil, then reduce heat & simmer for 3-4 mins before the sauce becomes thickened & reduced. There will not be a lot of moisture left.

7. Divide cauliflower rice with ground beef into plates. Garnish with grated onion, sesame seeds, & slices of cucumber.

Carne Asada & Marinade

(Ready in about 15 mins | Serving 6 | Difficulty: Easy)

Per serving: kcal: 340, Fat: 21g, Net Carbs: 2g, Protein: 32g

Ingredients

- Minced medium Jalapeno 1

- Minced Garlic cloves 4

- Fresh chopped cilantro ½ c

- Lime juice 6 tbsp

- Olive oil 6 tbsp

- Cumin 1 tsp

- Sea salt 1&1/2 tsp

- Black pepper ½ tsp

- Flank steak 2 lb.

Instructions

1. Inside a Whisk Ware Dressing Shaker, whisk together all of the carne asada marinade components (all but the steak).
2. Put the steaks on a glass baking platter in a single sheet. Pour over the steaks with the marinade & transform to cover.
3. Cover with a wrap of plastic, & cool for 2-8 hrs. (If you do this any longer, the meat might get mushy.)
4. Heat carne asada using an oven-followed grill plate-use this method for cooking steak in the oven.
5. Rest against the grain for five minutes, and after that, slice finely.

Low-Carb Keto Taco Soup

(Ready in about 20 mins | Serving 8 | Difficulty: Easy)

Per serving: kcal: 309, Fat: 24g, Net Carbs: 6g, Protein: 13g

Ingredients

- Ground beef 1 lb.

- Taco seasoning 3 tbsp

- Beef bone broth 3 c

- 2 cans Diced Tomatoes (14.5 oz)

- RANCH DRESSING ¾ C

Instructions

1. Brown the ground beef in the bottom of a big pot over medium-high heat for around 7-10 minutes, until it is no longer pink. Drain if you do.

2. Apply 2 spoonfuls (28 g) of taco seasoning (2/3 of the total) and 3/4 cup (177 mL) of broth. Simmer for several minutes, before much of the liquid is gone.

3. Include the remaining broth, sliced tomatoes (with liquid), plus remaining spoonful of taco seasoning. Swirl. Bring to a moderate boil, and steam for around 8-10 mins.

4. Remove from heat. Wait for two minutes, then mix in dressing for the field. Garnish with melted cheddar cheese & coriander if needed.

Lasagna Stuffed Spaghetti Squash Boats with Meat – Low Carb

(Ready in about 55 mins | Serving 7 | Difficulty: Medium)

Per serving: kcal: 287, Fat: 22g, Net Carbs: 8g, Protein: 14g

Ingredients

Spaghetti squash

- Medium Spaghetti squash 1

- Olive oil 4 tsp

- Sea salt>> to taste

Meat layer

- Olive oil 1 tbsp

- Garlic cloves 2

- Ground beef ½ lb.

- Sea salt ½ tsp

- Black pepper 1/8 tsp

- Marinara sauce ½ c

- Italian seasoning 1 tsp

Cheese layers

- Ricotta cheese 2/3 c

- Grated parmesan cheese 1/3 c

- Olive oil 1 tbsp

- Sea salt>> to taste

- Shredded Mozzarella cheese 2/3 c

Instructions

Spaghetti squash

1. Heat the spaghetti squash inside the oven at 425 °
   F (218 ° C) as described here.

Meat layer

1. In the meantime, heat the rest of the tablespoon of oil over medium-high heat in a large skillet. Add the garlic & roast, until fragrant, for around 30 seconds. Stir in the ground beef. Season with black pepper and sea salt. Cook until browned, splitting apart the meat with either a spoon or spatula (about 10 minutes).

2. Stir in Italian seasoning and marinara sauce. Reduce heat to a medium simmer. Simmer for 10 minutes, approximately. If the squash is prepared before it's finished, cover to stay warm.

Ricotta *parmesan cheese layer*

1. In a big cup, whisk the ricotta cheese & parmesan cheese as well as a tablespoon of olive oil together. (The bowl should be wide enough later to incorporate the strands of spaghetti squash.) Set aside.

Assembly

1. When frying, take the spaghetti squash out of the oven but keep it on at 425 °F (218 ° C).
2. Split the squash halfway down the duration. Place the side open into the baking dish & use a fork to remove threads.
3. Placed the spaghetti squash threads with the ricotta & parmesan cheeses into the wide tub. Blend in. Season to taste, with sea salt.
4. Pack the mixture of spaghetti squash back into the hollow shells at the baking tray. Cover with a mixture of beef marinara. Sprinkle over with sliced mozzarella.
5. Send the spaghetti lasagna squash boats to the oven for about ten minutes before the cheese melts.

Ground Beef Cabbage Soup – Instant Pot or Crock Pot

(Ready in about 4 hrs. 15 mins | Serving 14 | Difficulty: Hard)

Per serving: kcal: 111, Fat: 6g, Net Carbs: 4g, Protein: 9g

Ingredients

- Avocado oil 1 tbsp

- Large chopped Onion 1

- Ground beef 1lb.

- Sea salt 1 tsp

- Black pepper ¼ tsp

- Shredded coleslaw mix, 1 lb.

- 1 can Diced Tomatoes (15 oz)

- Beef bone broth 6 c

- 1 tbsp Italian seasoning 1 tbsp

- Garlic powder ½ tsp

- Medium Bay leaf 2

Crockpot cabbage soup - slow cooker

Instructions

1. Heat the oil over medium heat in a big, sauté pan. Stir in the sliced onions. Cook, stirring regularly, for around 10-15 minutes before the onions begin to smoke.

2. Apply ground beef to the saucepan. Season with black pepper and sea salt. Growing temperatures to medium-high. Cook for around 7-10 minutes, splitting apart with a spatula, until the beef is browned.

3. In the meanwhile put the remaining ingredients in the Crock-Pot.

4. Once the beef is golden brown, add the combination of beef and onions to the Crock-Pot. Stir to blend. Season with extra salt and/or pepper to compare.
5. Cook on low for 5-6 hours, or high for 2-3 hours. Remove the leaves from the bay before eating.

Instant pot cabbage soup - pressure cooker

Instructions

1. On Instant Pot, click the Sauté key. Stir in the oil and cut the onions. Cook, stirring regularly, for around 10-15 mins, before the onions begin to smoke.
2. Instant Cooker of ground beef. Season with black pepper and sea salt. Increase the sauté to "Strong" temperature Cook for around 7-10 minutes, splitting apart with a spatula, until the beef is cooked through.

3. Switch off the heat when the beef is cooked and add the rest of the ingredients to the Instant Cooker. Stir to blend. Season to match with more salt and/or pepper.

4. Cover Instant Pot and lock it. Click the button File and set the duration to 20 mins. When the cooking is complete, let the pressure relax for 5 minutes naturally and then use fast release. Remove bay leaves before eating.

Gluten-Free Tamale Pie Casserole

(Ready in about 30 mins | Serving 12 slices | Difficulty: Easy)

Per serving: kcal: 313, Fat: 26g, Net Carbs: 3.5g, Protein: 15g

Ingredients

- Olive oil 1 tsp

- 1 recipe Almond flour pie crust

- Minced garlic cloves 3

- Ground beef 1 lb.

- Sea salt 1 tsp

- Black pepper ½ tsp

- 1 can green chiles (4 oz)

- Gluten-free enchilada sauce ½ c

- Shredded Cheddar cheese 1 c

- Fresh cilantro

Instructions

1. If you don't use store-bought enchilada sauce, create homemade gluten-free enchilada sauce as guided here.

2. Create the savory almond flour pie crust as described in here. (Remove from oven when everything is finished and keep the oven on at 350 ° F (177 ° C).

3. In the meanwhile, heat oil over low heat in a skillet. Add garlic, and sauté until fragrant, for a min.

4. Transfer ground beef to the saucepan. Season with black pepper and sea salt. Increases temperature to moderate-high. Cook for 7-10 minutes before the beef is browned and fat burns down, breaking off with either a spoon or spatula. (If the beef is browned, however, the liquid is still intact, remove it before proceeding.)

5. Stir in green chiles and enchilada sauce until the beef is cooked clean. Cook 3 more mins.

6. Move the meat mixture into the baked pie crust uniformly and pinch the end. Sprinkle over with melted cheese. Bake for ten minutes, until molten cheese. If needed, garnish with cilantro

Garlic Herbs Butter with Filet Mignon

(Ready in about 15 mins | Serving 8 | Difficulty: Easy)

Per serving: kcal: 350, Fat: 29g, Net Carbs: 0.16g, Protein: 20g

Ingredients

- Butter 2tbsp

- Fresh rosemary ½ tbsp

- Fresh thyme ½ tbsp

- Minced garlic clove 1

- Filet mignon (8 oz)

- Sea salt>>to taste

- Black pepper>>to taste

Instructions

1. Put half of the butter together (1 tbsp, 14 g), rosemary, thyme, and garlic. (Sprinkle with a slight amount of sea salt while using unsalted butter.) Form into a log and cool before the last phase.

2. To 400 °F, preheat the oven.

3. Trim some connective tissue along beef tenderloin margins. The filets are liberally seasoned on both sides with salt & black pepper.

4. In medium-high pressure, pressure the cast iron skillet until the skillet is heavy. Melt the rest of the butter in the skillet (1 tablespoon, 14 g).

5. Add those fillets. Sear on either hand for two minutes, without turning them anymore.

6. Move the skillet to the oven, which is preheated. Bake for ideal doneness stage. For a 2 in (5 cm) thick filet, that is five minutes for uncommon, 6 minutes for medium unusual, 7 minutes for medium-well, or 8 mins for medium good. Using a

meat thermometer to verify the correct temperature for medium well-125 °F (52 °C) for normal, 130 °F (54 °C) for medium fine, 140 °F (60 °C) for average, and 155 °F (68 °C). The temperature rises by an additional 5 degrees F when resting.

7. Take the filets from the oven and move to a tray. Cover each one of them with 1/2 tbsp (7 g) of herb butter (cut the butter log into four pieces and place one on each steak). Before cutting, let steaks rest for 5 mins.

Low-Carb - Hunan Beef

(Ready in about 12 mins | Serving 4 | Difficulty: Easy)

Per serving: kcal: 317, Fat: 21g, Net Carbs: 4g, Protein: 24g

Ingredients

- Coconut aminos 2 tbsp

- Sherry cooking wine 2 tbsp

- Arrowroot powder 1 tbsp

- Flank steak 1 lb.

- Avocado oil 3 tbsp

- Crushed Dried Thai chile peppers 2

- Minced garlic cloves 2

- Ground ginger ½ tsp

- Black pepper ¼ tsp

Instructions

1. Stir the coconut aminos, cooking water, and arrowroot powder together in a medium dish. Attach the sliced beef to brush and flip. Put back for 30 minutes to marinate.

2. Heat avocado oil to high heat in a broad wok. Stir the beef in and fry for almost a min.

3. Connect Thai chili peppers, sliced garlic, ground ginger & black pepper. Fry for another minute.

4. Serve with cooked broccoli (please cut out the Parmesan). Where appropriate, garnish with chives & sesame seeds.

Low-Carb Keto Meatballs - Italian Style

(Ready in about 30 mins | Serving 6 | Difficulty: Easy)

Per serving: kcal: 324, Fat: 22g, Net Carbs: 4g, Protein: 25g

Ingredients

- Grated parmesan cheese ¼ c

- Sunflower seed meal ¼ c

- Italian seasoning 1 tbsp

- Sea salt ¾ tsp

- Black pepper ½ tsp

- Unsweetened coconut milk beverage ¼ c

- Grated Onion 3 tbsp

- Large Egg 1

- Minced garlic cloves 3

- Fresh chopped parsley 2 tbsp

- Ground beef 1 lb.

- Marinara sauce ¾ c

Instructions

1. To 425 ° F preheat the oven. Cover a baking sheet with foil or parchment paper (grease by using foil).
2. Mix the sunflower seed meal, grated Parmesan cheese, Italian seasoning, marine salt & black pepper in a wide dish.
3. In the milk, whisk the onion, potato, garlic, & fresh parsley, grated. Let the mixture settle in for a few minutes.
4. Using your hands to blend the ground beef so it is all mixed. (Don't over-mix to remove rough meatballs.)
5. Form the mixture into balls of 1 in (2,5 cm) and put it on the lined baking sheet. (A little scoop of cookies fits great for this. Use a soft touch by using

your hands, and don't stack the meatballs very tightly.)

6. Bake for 10-12 mins, until only the meatballs are cooked. (If you like them more golden, you should bring them under the broiler for a few minutes.)

7. Top with a marinara sauce for each meatball. Return to the oven and bake until the sauce is heated, and the meatballs are cooked through for 3-5 minutes. Garnish with newly added parsley.

Paleo Keto Low-Carb Meatloaf

(Ready in about 1 hr. 10 mins | Serving 12 | Difficulty: Easy)

Per serving: kcal: 215, Fat: 14g, Net Carbs: 3g, Protein: 17g

Ingredients

- Ground beef 2 lb.

- Golden flaxseed meal ½ c

- Diced large Onion 1/2

- Minced garlic cloves 8

- Tomato paste 3 oz

- Worcestershire sauce 2 tbsp

- Large Eggs 2

- Italian seasoning 1 tbsp

94

- Sea salt 2 tsp

- Black pepper ½ tsp

- Sugar-free ketchup 1/3 c

Instructions

1. To 350 ° F preheat the oven. Grease a loaf pan 9x5 in (23x13 cm) and put aside.
2. Combine all ingredients in a big tub, save for ketchup. Mix once fully blended, so do not over-mix.
3. The mixture is poured into the loaf tub. Bake 30 minutes.
4. Pour the ketchup (if using) over the meatloaf. Return to the oven and bake for another 25-45 minutes until cooked through & internal temp exceeds 160 ° F (71 ° C). (The period varies according to loaf thickness.)
5. Stop slicing for 10 minutes. Using a serrated bread knife to cut carefully.

Instant Pot Steak Fajita

(Ready in about 12 mins | Serving 4 | Difficulty: Easy)

Per serving: kcal: 256, Fat: 12.5g, Net Carbs: 6.2g, Protein: 26.8g

Ingredients

- Skirt steak 1 lb.

- Fajita seasoning mix 2 tbsp

- Avocado oil 1 tbsp

- sliced large Bell peppers 2

- sliced medium Onion 1

- Beef bone broth ½ c

- Lime juice 2 tbsp

Instructions

1. Toss steak into a fajita seasoning tablespoon.

2. Press the "Sauté" button on the Instant Pot & adjust the temperature to "More" (by repeatedly pressing "Sauté" until "More" is displayed on the screen. In a single layer, add one spoonful of oil & 1/2 the steak. Sauté the steak for about 1-2 mins per side, not to cook completely but only to brown. Remove and repeat the same with the remaining steak. Add the steak, which was cooked back to the pot, from the first lot.

3. Add vegetables & sprinkle with unused seasoning for the fajita. Stir in vegetables to cover in seasoning if necessary. Add the lime juice & the broth.

4. Close the lid and close the vent from the sealing position. Press the "Manual" button & set High Pressure to two minutes. Use Quick Release to immediately relieve pressure.

Ground Beef Pesto Zucchini Stir Fry

(Ready in about 20 mins | Serving 6 | Difficulty: Easy)

Per serving: kcal: 468.1, Fat: 37.6g, Net Carbs: 2.9g, Protein: 30.7g

Ingredients

- Ground beef 1 lb.

- Sea salt 1 tsp

- Black pepper ½ tsp

- Sliced medium Zucchini 2

- Minced Garlic cloves 2

- Basil pesto ¾ c

- Goat cheese ½ c

- Freash chopped parsley 2tbsp

Instructions

1. Cook the minced garlic in a frying pan over medium heat for about a minute until it is fragrant.
2. Add the ground beef. Sprinkle on to taste with salt & pepper. Increase to medium heat. Cook 7-10 minutes until browned, breaking apart with either a spoon or spatula.
3. Add some zucchini. Cook for 5-7 mins, occasionally stirring until the zucchini begins to soften & turn golden.
4. Remove from heat. Add basil pesto. Toss with the parsley & goat cheese.

Keto Eggplant Easy Lasagna

(Ready in about 60 mins | Serving 8 | Difficulty: Easy)

Per serving: kcal: 426, Fat: 30g, Net Carbs: 6g, Protein: 30g

Ingredients

Meat sauce

- Olive oil 1 tsp

- Minced Garlic cloves 2

- Ground beef 1&1/2 lb.

- Sea salt 1 tsp

- Black pepper ½ tsp

- Marinara sauce 1&1/2 c

- Italian seasoning 1 tbsp

Roasted eggplant

- sliced Eggplant 20 oz

- Olive oil 2 tbsp

- Sea salt>>to taste

- Black pepper>> to taste

Cheese filling

- Ricotta cheese 8 oz

- Grated parmesan cheese ½ c

- large Egg 1

Cheese topping

- Mozzarella cheese 2 cup

Instructions

Roasted eggplant

1. To 400 °F Oven preheats. Line a baking tray, & grease it.

2. Organize the eggplant slices on a large baking tray (or 2 smaller ones) in a single layer. Brush with olive oil, both sides. Season with pepper & sea salt.

3. Bake the eggplant in the oven, until soft, for about 15 to 25 mins. Remove from the oven when done & leave the oven on at 400 °F (204 ° C).

Meat sauce

1. While eggplant is roasting over medium-high heat, heat oil in a large saucepan. Connect the garlic & roast, until fragrant, for around 30 seconds. Stir in ground beef. Season with pepper as well as sea salt. Cook until browned, breaking apart the meat with the use of a spoon or spatula (about ten minutes).

2. Stir in Italian seasoning and marinara sauce. Lower the heat to a mild simmer. Simmer for 10 minutes, about.

Cheese filling

1. Make cheese filling, whereas meat sauce simmers. Stir the ricotta cheese, the Parmesan cheese, and the egg in a small bowl.

Assembly

1. Line the bottom of a 9x13 in (23x33 cm) glass or casserole stoneware platter with a roasted eggplant slices single layer (typically 6 slices for one layer). Top with a mixture of ground beef marinara. Spread over the ricotta mixture. Sprinkle shredded mozzarella cheese. Again, repeat the layers with the last shredded cheese.
2. Bake 10-15 mins, until the top cheese is melted as well as golden.

Keto Lasagna Without Noodles

(Ready in about 40 mins | Serving 8 | Difficulty: Easy)

Per serving: kcal: 355, Fat: 25g, Net Carbs: 5g, Protein: 24g

Ingredients

- Ground beef 1 lb.

- Sea salt 1/8 tsp

- Black pepper 1 dash

- Whole milk ricotta cheese 1&1/2 c

- Grated parmesan cheese ½ c

- Marinara sauce 25 oz

- Mozzarella cheese 8 oz

Instructions

1. To 350 ° F preheat the oven.
2. The ground beef is seasoned with salt and black pepper.
3. Over medium heat, heat a large skillet. Add the beef and cook, stirring with a wooden spoon and breaking the meat until browned. Drain away any excess fat.
4. Move the beef to a baking pan with a 9x9 inch bottom.
5. Scattered the ricotta over the top, then the Parmesan. Then pour over the layers with the marinara sauce & top with mozzarella.
6. Bake for 25 mins, until the top cheese melts and browns.

Keto Low-Carb Ground Beef Stroganoff

(Ready in about 30 mins | Serving 6 | Difficulty: Easy)

Per serving: kcal: 378.9, Fat: 29.1g, Net Carbs: 4.8g, Protein: 24.5g

Ingredients

- Olive oil 2 tbsp

- Sliced large Onion 1/2

- Sliced Cremini mushrooms 8 oz

- Ground beef 1 lb.

- Sea salt ½ tsp

- Black pepper ¼ tsp

- Minced Garlic cloves 2

- Beef bone broth 1 c

- Coconut amino 2 tbsp

- Sour cream ½ c

- Cream cheese 2 oz

Instructions

1. Heat olive oil over medium heat in a large saucepan pan. Add onions & mushroom. Sauté until the onions & mushrooms are tender but also brown, & extra fluid has evaporated for about ten minutes.

2. Boost the heat to medium-high. Push mushrooms & onions to the corners & add the ground beef to the middle of the saucepan, as well as a season with salt & pepper. Cook for 8-10 mins, stirring occasionally & breaking the beef apart until the beef is cooked through. Once it starts cooking a bit, you can stir it with the chestnuts and onions.

3. Make a well in the middle & add the chopped garlic. Sauté the meat for about a min, until it is fragrant, then stir in.

4. Add aminos to the bone broth & coconut, if used. Bring to a boil and simmer for five mins until most of the fluid is diminished but little remains.
5. Add sour cream & cream cheese until it is smooth.
6. Serve with over spaghetti squash.

Keto Low-Carb Philly Cheesesteak Casserole

(Ready in about 30 mins | Serving 6 | Difficulty: Easy)

Per serving: kcal: 689.7, Fat: 48.9g, Net Carbs: 7.2g, Protein: 52.5g

Ingredients

- Ground beef 2 lb.

- Sea salt 2 tsp

- Black pepper ½ tsp

- sliced large Bell peppers 3

- sliced large Onion 1

- Italian seasoning ½ tbsp

- Smoked paprika 1 tsp

- Garlic powder ½ tsp

- Cream cheese 4 oz

- Chicken bone broth ¼ c

- Provolone cheese 6 slices

Instructions

1. To 350 ° F preheat the oven.
2. Place the beef over medium-high heat in a large sauté pan and break with a spatula. Season with pepper & sea salt. Cook, occasionally stirring, for 8-10 mins until browned & cooked through.
3. Put bell peppers & onions into the saucepan. Seasoning with Italian, paprika, & garlic powder. Sauté, until vegetables are tender, for 10-15 mins.
4. Add broth and cream cheese. Mix until it is melted & smooth.
5. shift the mixture to a large baking dish made of stoneware (8 x 11 ½). Arrange slices of provolone on top, slightly overlapping.
6. Bake for 10 to 15 mins, until cheese is melted.

Keto Low-Carb Cheesy Tacos Skillet

(Ready in about 25 mins | Serving 4 | Difficulty: Easy)

Per serving: kcal: 547, Fat: 35g, Net Carbs: 12g, Protein: 41g

Ingredients

- Ground beef 1 lb.

- Taco seasoning 2 tbsp

- Water ½ c

- Diced large Onion 1/2

- Sliced large Bell peppers 3

- 1 can of Diced tomatoes of 14.5 oz

- Mexican cheese blend 1 c

- Sliced Green onions ¼ c

Instructions

1. Heat skillet over moderate to high heat. Add the ground beef and cook for about ten minutes until browned, breaking the beef apart with a spatula or spoon.

2. Add water and taco seasoning. Cook for two-three minutes until it absorbs or evaporates the excess water.

3. Reduce to medium heat. Add the bell peppers and the onions. Cook for 5-10 mins, until the onions are translucent and soft.

4. Stir in the chopped tomatoes. Simmer for several minutes, until heat evaporates as well as any excess moisture.

5. Reduce to low heat. Sprinkle over with shredded cheese. Cover the pan and heat until the cheese has melted. Remove the green onions from heat, and top.

Keto No-Rice Cabbage Rolls

(Ready in about 60 mins | Serving 6 | Difficulty: Medium)

Per serving: kcal: 321, Fat: 18g, Net Carbs: 10g, Protein: 25g

Ingredients

- Head Cabbage 1

- Ground beef 1 lb.

- 1 can of diced tomatoes (14.5 oz)

- Large Egg 1

- Minced Garlic cloves 4

- Italian seasoning 2 tsp

- Sea salt 1 tsp

- Black pepper ¼ tsp

- Cauliflower rice 1 c

- 1 can of Tomato sauce (15 oz)

Instructions

1. To 350 ° F preheat the oven.
2. Bring a big saucepan of water to boil. Add the cabbage head in the boiling water and fully immerse it. Boil for 5-8 mins, until the leaves bend softly enough. They're going to turn greenish & the outer leaves could come off, which is all right so you can take them out.
3. Remove the chives from boiling water. Place aside to freshen up. For now, leave the warm water in the pot. You might want it later when you peel the leaves of the cabbage.
4. Meanwhile, as per the guidelines here, stir fry cauliflower rice for several minutes.
5. Mix the ground beef, finely chopped tomatoes, egg, minced garlic, Italian seasoning, salt, and black pepper in a large bowl. Mix until just put together, do not over-mix. Fold in cooked rice with cauliflower. Place aside.
6. In a large, rectangle, or oval ceramic baking sheet, spread 1/2 the tomato sauce. Set aside.

7. Cautiously peel out the cabbage leaves. To do this, flip over the core side as well as cut the leaves from the core one-by-one, then peel carefully. Instead of peeling the leaves behind, slide one's fingers between the cabbage layers to release them. The outside leaves will be soft & easier to peel but may be firmer inside. If they're too firm & crisp to bend, the slightly peeled cabbage may be returned to boiling water with a few more mins to soften more.

8. Cut thick rib from the middle of every cabbage leaf & cut in "V" form. Through 1 end of a cabbage leaf, place 1/3 c (67 grams) of beef combination into a log shape. Fold in sides, & then roll up like a burrito. Place the roll of cabbage, seam side down, over the sauce & into the baking platter. Repeat to make twelve rolls with cabbage. (If the internal leaves are very small, you might need to overlap them with two to fit the filling.)

9. Sprinkle over cabbage rolls with the rest of the tomato sauce. Cover the baking tray with foil tightly for one hour or until the beef is baked through.

Keto Corned Beef & Cabbage in the Pressure Cooker

(Ready in about 1 hr. 30 mins | Serving 12 | Difficulty: Medium)

Per serving: kcal: 433, Fat: 33g, Net Carbs: 6g, Protein: 25g

Ingredients

Corned beef and cabbage:

- Corned beef brisket 4 lb.

- Beef bone broth 2 c

- Large head Cabbage 1

- Large Onions 2

- Celery root 1 lb.

- Sea salt>>to taste

- Black pepper>> to taste

Horseradish sauce:

- Sour cream ¾ c

- Mayonnaise ½ c

- Prepared horseradish ¼ c

- Lemon juice 2 tsp

- Garlic powder ½ tsp

Instructions

1. Unwrap the brisket of corned beef & set aside packet to season. Rinse, under cold water, corned beef, then pat dry. (It's going to be salty if you don't wash it.) cut any belly weight from the brisket if you prefer. That's up to you as fat isn't a keto problem. At least leave about one-fourth inch of fat for taste.

2. In the 10 QT Crock-Pot Express Easy Steam Release Pressure Cooker, place the brisket, fat side

upwards. Sprinkle over the brisket the seasonings from the packet and press gently to help them stick.

3. To avoid harming the seasonings, spill beef bone broth in to pressure cooker, from around brisket but not over it.

4. Cover & turn to seal the lid. Press Manual Pressure & increase time to 1 hr. 15 mins. Press Launch. Use Quick Release when time runs out to release the pressure. Once no steam exits, open the lid.

5. In the meantime, stir the ingredients of horseradish sauce together. In the fridge, cover and chill until the corned beef is fully prepared.

6. Once the pressure cooker lid is opened, add the diced onion, celery root, & cabbage to the broth around the beef in that order (the cabbage ought to be on top). The cabbage is gently seasoned with pepper and salt.

7. Cover and cook for 15 more mins again on high pressure. Enable pressure to release slowly, which takes about ten minutes, and use Quick Release afterward.

8. Cut the corned beef into the half-inch slices or, if desired, move it to a roasting pan first and place it in the oven under the broiler for a few minutes until brown (optional).

9. Put sliced corned beef as well as cabbage (together with the onions & celery root) on a platter to serve. If desired, drizzle with liquid to cook. Serve with sauce of horseradish.

Keto Low-Carb Tacos Casserole

(Ready in about 2 hrs. 15 mins | Serving 6 | Difficulty: Medium)

Per serving: kcal: 612, Fat: 43g, Net Carbs: 4g, Protein: 48g

Ingredients

Taco casserole:

- Avocado oil 1 tbsp

- Ground beef 2 lb.

- Water ¾ c

- Taco seasoning ¼ c

- Diced large Bell peppers 2

- Diced large Onion 1/4

- 2 cans of Diced tomatoes of 10 oz with green chiles

- Cheddar cheese 1 c

Optional toppings:

- Shredded Iceberg lettuce

- Fresh diced tomatoes

- Cubed Avocados

- Fresh chopped cilantro

- Sour cream

Instructions

1. Heat avocado oil in a large saucepan pan over medium to high flame. Put in the ground beef. Cook 8-10 mins, breaking apart by a spatula until browned.
2. Include the taco seasoning & water. Bring to a peak, then cook for 2-5 mins before the meat thickens & shapes a taco.

3. Move the beef to a Cook & Bring a Simple Tidy Slow Cooker Seven QT Crock-Pot. Add the chopped peppers, onions, & green chilies to drained, chopped tomatoes. Blend Everything.

4. Cover the cap of the slow cooker and cook Low for four hours or Fast for 2-3 hours. At this stage, you can take your Cook & Bring Crock-Pot anywhere you need to (use side latches to close the lid), and only connect it in to keep it warm until you get there.

5. Stir the saucepan straight before eating. (You should spoon out some extra liquid that might have collected, but if you've drained the tomatoes properly, there shouldn't be much.) set Crock-Pot slow cooker to Maximum and scatter the shredded cheese on top. Cover and simmer, before the cheese, melt, for around 5 minutes.

6. Cover your casserole with some broccoli, onions, avocados, and cilantro toppings you want.

Garlic Butter Rib Prime Roast

(Ready in about 1 hr. 15 mins | Serving 20 | Difficulty: Medium)

Per serving: Cal: 575, Fat: 51g, Protein: 24g

Ingredients

- 4-bone Standing rib roast 1

- Sea salt 1&1/2 tbsp

- Black pepper 1 tsp

- Butter 6 tbsp

- Italian seasoning 2 tbsp

- Minced Garlic cloves 10 (minced; about 10-12 cloves or 5-6 tsp minced)

Instructions

1. Put the fatty side upside down prime rib into a roasting pan equipped with a roasting rack. Freely season with salt and pepper. Leave it to rest for 1 hour at room temp.

2. To 450 °F preheat the oven.

3. Mix butter, Italian seasoning & chopped garlic in a shallow bowl. Pour the paste on the prime rib, then apply uniformly with a basting brush.

4. In the oven, uncovered, roast the prime rib for 20 - 30 mins, until the garlic on top is golden brown, but it's not burnt. Tent on top of prime rib with foil. Lessen oven temp to 350 ° F (176 ° C) and proceed to roast until the target internal temp exceeds the prime rib:

   110 F (43 C) for unusual-55 to 65 minutes or so

   115 F (46 C) medium rare-60 to 70 minutes approx.

   Medium 125 F (51 C)-around 65-80 minutes

   It would take around an average 8 to 9 mins per pound of beef at 350 ° F (176 ° C) for medium fresh, after the original high-temper roast at 450

°F (232 ° C). The meat temperatures described above are not ultimate temperatures, only the temperature to achieve in the oven. In the next stage, the interior temperature would increase by another 20 °.

5. The prime rib is extracted from the oven. Let it rest another 20 mins before slicing, to arrive at the right temp and finish frying.

KETOGENIC DIET

SIDE DISHES COOKBOOK

SIDE DISHES

Keto Spaghetti Squash Casserole

(Ready in about 35 mins |Serving 6| Difficulty: Easy)

Per serving: Kcal 168, Fat:13g, Net Carbs:4g Protein:8g

Ingredients

- Spaghetti squash cooked 2 cups

- Egg 1

- Herbs de Provence 1 tsp

- Onion & chive cream flavored cheese 8 oz

- Pinch of salt

- Mozzarella cheese 1 cup

Instructions

1. Oven preheated to 350.
2. Liquid the baking spray in a baking dish. Place the baked spaghetti vegetables in the dish.
3. In a quick processor, add the milk, cream cheese, herbs & salt. Mix until smooth. Pour it over the vegetable spaghetti.
4. Scatter of cheese over it. Bake until white, for thirty to forty mins.

Garlicky Green Beans Stir Fry

(Ready in about 25 mins |Serving 4| Difficulty: Easy)

Per serving: Cal 171, Fat:7g, Net Carbs:8.5g Protein:6g

Ingredients

- Fresh green beans 1 lb.

- Peanut oil 2 t

- Chopped garlic 2 t

- Yellow onion 1/2 small

- Salt 1/4 tsp

- oyster sauce 2 t

Instructions

1. Cut green beans on both sides.
2. Slice the green beans into 2-inch pieces, wash and spin dry with paper towels in the salad spinner (affiliate link). (Beans bought do not need to wash.)
3. Heat the wok or a large frying pan over high heat for 1-2 minutes, before your hand is too hot to stay over it.
4. Add the oil and boil for around 30 seconds, then add the slivers of garlic and onion, and simmer for 20-30 seconds, stirring the entire time.
5. Connect beans and salt and cook, stirring many times, for around 2 minutes.
6. Then add hot, cover wok, and let steam beans for five minutes. (I tested once to see if the pan appeared dry and applied around 1 tsp. more water.)

7. Uncover the pan and apply the oyster sauce, then cook for another 2 minutes, stirring so that all the beans are completely coated with the sauce.

8. When they're finished, beans can always be slightly crisp. Serve wet.

9. This can be stored for a day or two in the refrigerator and reheated in the oven, although you'll still have a little leftover.

Roasted Asparagus with Garlic, Lemon, & Parmesan

(Ready in about 15 mins |Serving 4| Difficulty: Easy)

Per serving: Cal 173, Fat:4g, Net Carbs:6g Protein:7g

Ingredients

- Asparagus 1 bunch

- Olive oil 3-4 tbsp

- Ground black pepper & Kosher salt

- Chopped garlic 2 cloves

- Grated Parmesan cheese 3 tbsp

- Juice of lemon 1/2

Instructions

1. Oven preheated to 425 °c.

2. Clean the garden asparagus & cut each stalk's bottom inch, get rid of the stiff, fibrous portion. It is a simple way to say when to cut to curve 1 asparagus stalk to the edge until it snaps away. Place it beside the remaining of the garden asparagus and split both of them to about the same weight.

3. Pat the garden asparagus to dry and scatter over a cookie sheet in a thin layer. Silt only with olive oil, then gently spray with flake salt & black pepper (fresh). Grant the asparagus a toss in the olive oil and seasoning to cover it uniformly, after which bake it in the oven for 8-10 mins, depending on size, until tender.

4. Take it from the oven & brush with garlic, Parmesan cheese, & lemon juice. Before eating, add another toss.

Fluffy Low-Carb Mashed Cauliflower with Celery Root (Keto)

(Ready in about 25 mins |Serving 6| Difficulty: Easy)

Per serving: Kcal 158, Fat:9g, Net Carbs:3g Protein:2g

Ingredients

- Cauliflower florets 1 pound

- Celeriac cubed & peeled 1 small

- Chopped garlic clove 1 large

- Heavy cream 1/3 cup

- Stick butter 1/2

- Salt & pepper

- Variations

- Add buttermilk for heavy cream

- Sub 1 lemon zest

- Top it with green onion

- Top it with minced parsley

- Top it with "bacon."

- Top it with fine cheddar

Instructions

1. **Celeriac:** Strip off the knob celery top & bottom. Then with a small knife & operating from top to bottom, cut the root as though you were about to supreme a grapefruit. Slice the knob celery into 1/2-inch slices, put the sliced garlic in a pot & cover with water. Carry the knob celery to a simmer & cook until soft, then pierce it quickly with a fork.

2. **Cauliflower:** Slice the cauliflower onto florets & put it in a bowl of microwavable. Apply two tbsp of water, cover & bake for 5 to 8 mins at high intensity or once the cauliflower is soft & pierced with such a fork.

3. **Puree:** put the cauliflower & knob celery (with garlic) in a mixing bowl & pulse the bits to separate. Apply the puree & whipping cream until smooth. Stir in butter, then blend properly. Garnish with pepper & salt. Then blend in the mash the chives.

Zucchini & Sweet Potato Latkes

(Ready in about 40 mins |Serving 1| Difficulty: Easy)

Per serving: Cal 122, Fat:9g, Net Carbs:6.25g Protein:3g

Ingredients

- Shredded zucchini 1 cup

- Shredded sweet potato 1 cup

- Beaten egg 1

- Coconut flour 1 tbsp

- Garlic powder 1/2 tsp

- Ground cumin 1/4 tsp

- Dried parsley 1/2 tsp

- Salt & pepper to taste

- Clarified butter 1 tbsp

- Extra virgin olive oil 1 tbsp

Instructions

1. In a med dish, add the courgette, sweet potato & egg.

2. Mix the coconut flour as well as the spices in a shallow bowl. Apply the courgette combination to the dry ingredients and blend until thoroughly mixed.

3. Heat the butter in a med non-stick skillet & the olive oil. Split the combination into 4 equal parts & fall into the saucepan. Push it down using a fork until a layer is shaped 1/2 inch thick. Cook until crispy & golden on med heat, then turn safely & bake the different side. Drop and drain onto a tray lined with tissue paper.

4. Top with an extra flake Salt. Serve warm

Grilling Zucchini

(Ready in about 25 mins |Serving 1| Difficulty: Easy)

Per serving: Cal 196, Fat:16g, Net Carbs:3.9g Protein:2g

Ingredients

- Two sliced zucchinis 10 to 12 inch long

- Vinaigrette salad 1/2 cup

- Garlic powder 1 tsp

Instructions

1. Break the courgette into pieces to guarantee the pieces are similar in thickness.
2. Mix your option of salad dressing, including garlic powder & dried herbs, if available.
3. Place the courgette pieces into the Ziploc container, add in the marinade and let the courgette marinate in the refrigerator for 4 hours or longer, or as long as needed for the entire day.

4. Drain the courgette into a colander put inside the sink until you are about to serve.

5. Heat it grills to med-high to roast courgette. If needed, you should spray your grill using a non-stick spray. However, the marinade does have plenty of oil, so you don't need it anyway.

6. Place the courgette diagonally on the grill pan, holding a spray bottle ready to tame any flames in the marinade that could rise from the grease.

7. Look for grill marks after 3-4 mins & if you see them move courgette heading the other way around. Cook 3 to 4 mins after you have gone spinning.

8. Switch the zucchini onto the other side & roast for some more mins or before the courgette starts to melt, with the exterior somewhat brown.

9. Top with pepper & salt fresh in the ground and serve warm.

Oven-Fried Parmesan Zucchini Rounds

(Ready in about 30 mins |Serving 12| Difficulty: Easy)

Per serving: kcal 71, Fat:4g, Net Carbs:3g Protein:6g

Ingredients

- 3 large zucchini, sliced (6 cups sliced rounds)

- 1 whole egg

- 1 egg white

- 1 1/2cups parmesan cheese, grated

- 1/4 cup fresh parsley, chopped

- 1/2 teaspoon garlic powder

- Olive oil cooking spray

Instructions

1. Oven preheated to 425oC.
2. Spray cookie sheets with baking Spray

3. Hit the egg white, set aside in a small bowl.

4. Put the Parmesan, parsley, and garlic powder in a different bowl and stir well.

5. Dip the Courgette in the mixture of the eggs, then in Parmesan, put it on the cookie sheet.

6. Don't cross courgettes on cookie dish.

7. Cook for ten mins, then turn them over and cook for ten mins, or until it becomes golden brown.

Keto Egg Fast Fettuccini Alfredo

(Ready in about 20 mins |Serving 1| Difficulty: Easy)

Per serving: kcal 491, Fat:47g, Net Carbs:2g Protein:19g

Ingredients

For the pasta:

- Eggs 2

- Cream cheese 1 oz

- Pinch salt

- Pinch of garlic powder

- Black pepper 1/8 tsp

For the sauce:

- Mascarpone cheese 1 oz

- Grated parmesan cheese 1 tbsp

- Butter 1 Tbsp

Instructions

For pasta:

1. In a grinder, add your eggs, cheese, cream, spice, garlic powder & pepper. Put into an 8 x 8 tray greased with butter. Bake eight minutes at 324 or before you just set. Remove& allow it to cool for five mins. Use a spatula to release the "pasta" sheet from the pan nicely. Turn it over and slice all into one/eight-inch thick pieces with a fine knife. Unroll softly, then put back.

For the sauce:

1. In a shallow cup, add the mascarpone, the parmesan cheese, and butter. 30 Second microwave on big. Click. Then click. Microwave another 30 seconds on big. Whisk until smooth again (this will take a minute since the sauce may be scattered-keep whisking, and it will come back together.) Add the pasta to the hot sauce and mix gently. Serve directly with freshly ground black pepper.

Grilled Eggplant Salad

(Ready in about 42 mins |Serving 6| Difficulty: Easy)

Per serving: Cal 183, Fat:10g, Net Carbs:23g Protein:4.3g

Ingredients:

- Thin Asian Eggplants 6

- Olive oil 1T to brush eggplants

- Fresh-& salty ground black pepper to season eggplants

- Grape tomatoes 1 cup

- Crumbled Feta 1/2 cup

Dressing ingredients:

- Fresh basil leaves 2/3 cup

- parsley leaves 1/3 cup

- large sliced garlic cloves 2

- Dijon mustard 1 t

- capers 3 t

- lemon juice 2 t

- additional-virgin olive oil 1/4 cup

Instructions

1. Heat up until med-high to BBQ.
2. Clean the aubergine if possible, then cut two ends. Cut the aubergine lengthwise, brown on both sides with olive oil, then top with salt & pepper upon its cut side
3. Put the cut side aubergine on your plate, then cook until you see some nice grill grates (about 5 to 7 mins).
4. Turn aubergine & cook for about five mins on the other hand, or until the aubergine is softened & very well browned.
5. Take the aubergine off from the cutting board & let It cool. Cut the tomatoes(grape) in half to make the beautiful dressing as the aubergine cool down.

6. Clean and turn as needed, dry out the basil & parsley leaves.

7. Choose the garlic cloves, then use a food processor with a steel blade to slice basil, peters, & ginger.

8. Apply the Dijon, capers, as well as lemon juice, then mix until the ingredients combine well; Now add the olive oil & stir it for thirty seconds.

9. Split it into pieces about one inch across, if the aubergine is treatable sufficiently.

10. Mix the aubergine & tomato halves nicely in a bowl and blend to coat the ingredients in a bread dressing (around 1/4 cup). For just another moment, save the remainder of dressing; too many things are perfect.

11. Apply a crumbled Feta & enjoy it.

Pan-Roasted Radishes (Low-Carb & Gluten-Free)

(Ready in about 60 mins | Serving 2| Difficulty: Easy)

Per serving: kcal 122, Fat:12g, Net Carbs:2.75g Protein:1g

Ingredients

- Quartered radishes 2 cups

- Butter 2 tbsp

- Lemon zest 1 tbsp

- Chopped chives 1 tbsp

- Pepper & salt to taste

Instructions

1. Melt the butter on a big, sauté pan. Apply the radishes, turn them down to protect. Cook over med heat for around ten mins, sometimes stirring

until its color changes to golden brown & softened. Remove it from heat and add the lemon zest & the chives. Top it with salt & pepper.

2. Alternatively, you should roast these in olive oil at 374 degrees (F) oven for about 35 mins. And add seasonings that you'd like.

Four Ingredient Sugar-Free Cranberry Sauce

(Ready in about 20 mins |Serving 8| Difficulty: Easy)

Per serving: Kcal 21, Fat:0g, Net Carbs:5g Protein:0g

Ingredients

- Bag of cranberries 12 oz

- Water 4 oz

- Trim healthy mama sweet 1 cup

- Vanilla 1 tsp

- Cinnamon 1 tsp

Instructions

1. Stir the cranberries as well as the water in a big saucepan. Cook for around 5 to 7 mins over med heat, until all the berries appear. Bring the rest of the ingredients together & lower the heat to med. Cook until needed fire. Might thicken further as it cools.

2. Put it in the freezer for about 2 weeks.

Pico de Gallo

(Ready in about 15 mins |Serving 6| Difficulty: Easy)

Per serving: Kcal 21, Net Carbs:6g Protein:1g

Ingredients

- Medium tomatoes 6
- Large onion 1
- Fresh cilantro leaves 1 cup
- Lime juice
- Salt

Instructions

1. Cut tomatoes, onion & cilantro into bits. Apply to a wide bowl, then whisk until mixed.
2. If you would like some fire, finely chop jalapeno and add to the bowl then.
3. Place in lime juice and season with salt.
4. Serve or chill before ready.

Low-Carb Onion Rings

(Ready in about 20 mins |Serving 4| Difficulty: Easy)

Per serving: Cal 175, Fat:16g, Net Carbs:4g Protein:3g

Ingredients

- Large onion 1

- Egg 1

- Coconut flour 2 tbsp

- Grated parmesan cheese 2 tbsp

- Garlic powder 1/8 tsp

- Parsley flakes 1/4 tsp

- Cayenne pepper 1/8 tsp

- Taste-salt
- Olive oil to fry 1/4 cup

Instructions

1. Heat the oil in a med pan.
2. In a small cup, smash the egg. In a small dish, mix the coconut flour with parmesan, garlic powder, parsley dust, cayenne, and spice.
3. Cut up the onion to around 1/2 to 3/4-inch-thick & split the rings, so you have a wide bunch. Apply all the onion rings to the egg mixture and completely blend so that they are fully covered. Drench the ointments in the egg for one minute, then move into the coating and then into the hot oil in small batches.
4. Fry until its color changes to a golden brown, then switch to brown the other side with a fork/tongs. To soak up some extra oil, drop to a plate lined with paper towels.
5. Serve with your favorite sauce (sugar-free).

Roasted Spicy Garlic Eggplant Slices

(Ready in about 30 mins |Serving 6| Difficulty: Easy)

Per serving: Kcal 64, Fat:5g, Net Carbs:5g Protein:1g

Ingredients

- Plant egg 1

- Olive oil 2 tbsp

- Garlic powder 1 tsp

- Red pepper 1/2 tsp

- Italian seasoning 1/2 tsp

- Salt 1 tsp

Instructions

1. Heat the oven to 425F.
2. Line a cookie sheet with a bakery release paper.
3. Cut the Aubergine into circles.
4. Place Aubergine slices in a single layer onto a cookie sheet.
5. Put olive oil on both sides of the Aubergine slices.
6. Sprinkle it with garlic powder, red pepper, sweet paprika & Italian seasoning on the Aubergine strips.
7. Place the aubergine in the oven & roast for 25 mins.
8. Aubergine extract from the oven and season with salt.

Roasted Baby Eggplant

(Ready in about 50 mins | Serving 16| Difficulty: Easy)

Per serving: Cal 44, Fat:4g, Net Carbs:1g Protein:1g

Ingredients

- Baby eggplant 1

- Olive oil 2 tbsp

- Kosher 1 tsp

- Ground pepper 1 tsp

- To serve:

- Ricotta cheese 1/3 cup

- Additional virgin olive oil 2 tbsp

- Ground pepper fresh

- Kosher to taste

Instructions

1. Clean the aubergine & slice it up. Place side up on a cutting baking sheet. Add the olive oil & season with fennel pollen, salt & pepper.

2. Bake for about forty-five mins in the 349 degrees (F) oven, or until softened & browned. Take away from the oven & let it cool. Serve warm.

3. Just before having to serve, top with roughly one tsp of cheese of ricotta for each half. Sprinkle with newly crushed peppercorns & just some grains of salt. Drizzle with olive oil of very good quality.

Crispy Fried Eggplant Rounds With Parmesan Cheese and Marinara Sauce

(Ready in about 30 mins |Serving 4| Difficulty: Easy)

Per serving: Kcal 233, Fat:17.26g, Net Carbs:7.15g
Protein:11.38g

Ingredients

- Eggplant 1 pound

- Crushed pork rinds 1 cup

- Grated parmesan cheese 1/2 cup

- Dried oregano 1 tsp

- Dried basil 1 tsp

- Salt 1/2 tsp

- Granulated garlic 1/4 tsp

- Onion Powder 1/4 tsp

- Pepper 1/4 tsp

- Beaten large eggs 2

- Olive oil 2 tbsp

Instructions

1. Prep: cut the aubergine into 10 to 12 rings, season with salt & place in such a colander for 15 mins to drain. Fully dry on tissue paper. In the meantime, in a small bowl, beat the eggs, big enough to hold an aubergine round & rush with a fork. In some other small bowl, whisk the pork rinds, cheese & season together. A tiny sheet of pan ready.

2. Procedure: Take around with the fork, then turn it back & forth into the egg until fully covered. Take a fork, then let the egg run away. Place the mixture into the breadcrumbs & cover with crumbs on top. Push the breadcrumbs upwards. Then turn the fork over the row and do it again. Round out the aubergine as well as a mix of the excess breadcrumbs. Lay it down on the sheet pan.

Repeat on all rounds of the procedure. Depending on how large they are, you should have plenty for 10 to 12 rounds.

3. Cook: Heat an iron pan over med-high heat. Alternatively, you can use a large pancake pan and fit everything on your pan at once. Once hot, add the oil. Add 3 to 4 round to your pan once the oil is hot, & now cook for three mins per side. Drain to a towel and then drain to a wire rack. You may have to put more oil to the pan as you go or just lower the heat a bit. The aubergine will be quite crispy & brown.

Artichoke with Herbed Mayonnaise

(Ready in about 40 mins |Serving 4| Difficulty: Easy)

Per Serving: kcal 245; protein 4.1g DV; carbs 12.5g fat 20.9g

Ingredients

- Artichokes 4

- Egg Yolks 2

- Dijon Mustard 1 Tsp

- Lemon Juice 4 Tsp

- Vegetable Oil 1 Cup

- Tarragon 1/4 Cup

- Salt

- Pepper

- Water

Instructions

1. Start by cutting the artichokes' outer leaves with scissors and separating the tops. Use a sharp knife to peel the stem's outer surface, as well as the artichoke's underside.

2. Carry a kettle of water to a boil and put the artichokes in such a steamer. Cook for around twenty mins, or until tender.

3. Have the mayonnaise, whereas the artichokes boil. Stir the egg yolks, vinegar, and lemon juice together. Apply a vegetable oil, then drizzle it slowly into combination while whisking hard. Thoroughly mix until the combination emulsifies & starts thickening. As desired, thin with water, then top with salt & pepper. Apply 1/4 tablespoon of newly herbs to top.

4. When steaming is finished, slice in half the artichokes and extract its choke with a blade.

5. Now happy to eat the artichokes. Eat by peeling off the leaf, dipping in the mayo, and scraping the teeth from the artichoke skin.

Spicy Stir-Fried Sugar Snap Peas

(Ready in about 25 mins |Serving 4| Difficulty: Easy)

Per serving: Cal 93, Fat:3.7g, Net Carbs:8.7g Protein:4.4g

Ingredients

- Sugar snap peas 1 lb.

- Soy sauce 2 t

- Sesame oil 1 tsp

- Sriracha sauce 1 tsp

- Fresh ginger root 3 slices

- Sliced garlic cloves 2 large

- Peanut oil 1 t

Instructions

1. By breaking the stem end & dragging its string down the foot, cut the ties from the sugars (glucose snap pea, then slice individual 1 on the diagonal.

2. Whisk the soy sauce/Soy Sauce Gluten-Free, sesame oil, as well as the Sriracha Sauce.

3. Place the wok on the grill/large frying pan, & preheat for 1 min.

4. Apply the oil once the wok is warm and let it run until the oil shines (approximately 15 to 30 sec depends on how warm the stove gets).

5. Apply the cut root & garlic ginger, then stir-fry only long enough to make them fragrant, add the oil, and cut.

6. Connect the cut sugar snap peas, then cook at high temperature, continuously stirring until the peas become bright green & then just start frying, around 2 mins.

7. Put within sauce combination & simmer for around 2 mins more, stirring continuously, before the sauce begins to cover the peas.

8. If desired, serve sweet, topped with Dark Sesame Seeds

Roasted Cabbage Wedges with Onion Dijon Sauce

(Ready in about 25 mins |Serving 4| Difficulty: Easy)

Per serving: Kcal 140, Fat:12.4g, Net Carbs:7.4g
Protein:1.8g

Ingredients

- Green cabbage 1/2 medium about 1½ pounds
- Garlic-infused olive-oil 1 tbsp
- Pepper & salt

Sauce:

- Butter 3 tbsp
- Chopped fresh onion 2 tablespoons
- Dijon mustard 1 tbsp
- Chopped garlic 1/2 tsp
- Each salt & pepper 1/8 tsp

168

Instructions

1. Preheat oven to 425 ° C. Line a cookie sheet with bakery release paper.

2. Split half of the cabbage into 4 equal slices & put on a ready cookie sheet. Using a pastry brush to cover each wedge's cut side with oil and top with salt pepper. Switch curtains & repeat.

3. In the oven, place the cookie sheet & cook for 10 to 12 mins. Turn the wedges & bake for another 8 to 10 mins more until it's browned.

4. In the meanwhile, apply together with all sauce ingredients to the tiny saucepan and simmer on med heat until the butter is thoroughly melted. Keep it warm.

5. Put the wedges on the tray to eat, mix sauce again, then chop over the wedges. Top it with parsley, or chives, if needed.

Roasted Salt & Pepper Radish Chips

(Ready in about 25 mins |Serving 4| Difficulty: Easy)

Per serving: Kcal 70, Fat:7.1g, Net Carbs:2.2g
Protein:0.4g

Ingredients

- Fresh radishes 16 ounce

- Coconut oil melted 2 tbsp

- Sea salt 1/2 tsp

- Pepper 1/2 tsp

Instructions

1. Oven preheated to 400 F.
2. Slice the radishes thinly.
3. Coat with oil.
4. Between 2 cookie sheets, spread radishes do not even overlap.
5. Then mix salt & pepper as well as scatter over the pieces.
6. Cook 12 to 15 mins.

Baked Artichoke Hearts Au Gratin

(Ready in about 1hour 10 mins |Serving 4| Difficulty: Easy)

Per serving: Cal 295, Fat:24g, Net Carbs:15g Protein:9g

Ingredients

- Frozen artichoke hearts one 12 oz, drained, thawed & larger cut in half

- Thinly sliced green onions 1/4 cup

- Olive oil 2 tsp

- Fresh & salty ground black pepper for taste

- Almond flour 1/4 cup

- Parmesan cheese 1/3 cup

- Pecorino Romano cheese 1/3 cup

- Dried thyme 1/2 tsp

172

- Dried oregano 1/4 tsp

- Mayo 1/3 cup

- Lemon zest 1 tsp

- Lemon juice 2 t

- Garlic puree 1/2 tsp

Instructions

1. Oven preheated to 324F/170 C.
2. If they're already frozen, thaw artichoke hearts in your oven and drain well.
3. Slice bigger artichoke heart in half lengthwise because it's the same size all around.
4. To grease 2 tiny gratin dishes/one med size baking dish, use olive oil.
5. Arrange a single sheet of artichoke hearts in the oiled bowl.
6. Then scatter on the artichokes with thinly chopped green onions, then top with salt & fresh black pepper.

7. Add the almond meal/flour, the Parmesan grated cheese, the pancetta-Romano grated cheese & the herbs.

8. Stir your mayo, lemon juice, lemon zest & garlic puree together, then blend into 1/2 cup cheese combination.

9. Using a rubber scraper to distribute it over the upper end of the artichoke core and set aside the remaining of the crumb or cheese bread combination.

10. Wrap the plates with paper, then bake 30 mins in a 324F/169C oven.

11. Take it from the oven and raise heat to 374F/190C.

12. Lift foil & top the leftover cheese combination.

13. Return to the oven & bake for around 25 mins or until the surface is mildly browned and the plate is hot clear.

14. Serve mild or hot.

Oven Roasted Basil Parmesan Tomatoes

(Ready in about 25 mins |Serving 6| Difficulty: Easy)

Per serving: Cal 60, Fat:2.67g, Net Carbs:4.3g

Ingredients

- Tomatoes 4

- Sea salt 1/2 tsp

- Garlic powder 1/2 tsp

- Onion Powder 1/2 tsp

- Dried oregano 1/2 tsp

- Black pepper 1/4 tsp

- Fresh small basil leaves 12

- Ground parmesan cheese 1/2 cup

Instructions

1. Oven preheated to 425 ° C. Line a rimmed cookie sheet with bakery release paper.

2. Cut the end of the tomatoes, then cut to thirds. If you choose a tomato that is bigger than a Roma, you are expected to get twice the number of slices.

3. Mix the salt, garlic powder, onion powder, oregano, & pepper in a shallow cup.

4. Place the slices of tomatoes over the bakery release paper in such a single layer. Sprinkle with seasoning blend both on sides of every slice.

5. Cover every slice of tomato with the basil leaf, & generously top every slice of grated parmesan.

6. Bake 15 to 20 mins once the cheese becomes golden brown & melted.

Mashed Cauliflower with Parmesan & Chives

(Ready in about 20 mins:| Serving 4-6 | Difficulty: Easy)

Per serving: Kcal 33 Fat 2g Carbs 1g Protein 3g

Ingredients

- Heads cauliflower cored 2 small & leaves removed & cut into small florets

- Chicken broth 2 cups

- Grated parmesan cheese 1/4 cup

- Fresh chopped chives 1/4 cup

- Ground black pepper & kosher salt

Instructions

1. Mix both cauliflower & chicken bouillon in a med saucepan & carry to a simmer.
2. Lower the heat to boil, cover it with a lid, then cook for 15-20 mins or when the cauliflower is soft but does not fall apart entirely.
3. Use a spoon with a slot to move the cauliflower to the mixing bowl and puree until smooth & silky.
4. Move to a dish, season with flake salt & ground black pepper, then mix in the Parmesan & minced chives. Serve hot.

Garlic Mashed Cauliflower

(Ready in about 22 mins :| Serving 4 | Difficulty: Easy)

Per serving: Kcal 101, Fat:9g, Net Carbs:3g Protein:2g

Ingredients

- Large cauliflower 1 divided in small florets

- Cream cheese low fat 3 ounces

- Salted butter 2 tbsp

- Minced garlic sautéed 1 1/2 teaspoon

Instructions

1. Carry a med kettle of water to simmer. The cauliflower is heated for eight to ten mins until it is cooked, or until the pork is soft. Remove cauliflower and wash.

2. Put cauliflower in a blender/food processor together with other ingredients, & pulse until smooth & fluffy.

Goat Cheese Cauliflower Bake Recipe

(Ready in about 30 mins :| Serving 8 | Difficulty: Easy)

Per serving: Cal 226, Fat:13g

Ingredients

- Large Cauliflowers 2 & chopped in 8 cups

- Hickory Smoked Bacon 4 strips

- Onion 1 cup

- Minced Garlic 4 tbsp

- Chopped Goat Cheese 10 ounces

- Low Fat softened Cream Cheese 1/4 cup

- Pepper & Salt to taste

- Sliced Green Onion for garnish

Instructions

1. Oven preheated to 400 ° F then spray the baking spray with a casserole bowl.

2. For 8 mins put the sliced cauliflower in a big bowl & microwave. Mix & microwave again for 8 mins before the fork-tender.

3. Heat a small skillet on med heat as cauliflower cooks, then cook the bacon until its color changes to a golden brown, around 2 to 3 mins on either side. Blotting the extra fat with a clean towel until fried, break it into tiny pieces and put aside. Make sure the bacon fat is stored inside the pan.

4. In med/high pressure, heat the reserved bacon fat & fry both onion & garlic until their color changes to golden brown and tender, only 2 to 3 mins.

5. Move the cooked cauliflower to a big mixing bowl, then substitute your cream cheese & the fried onions in 8 oz of chèvre. Run until well blended & nearly entirely smooth, with a few bits remaining in for texture.

6. Move the cauliflower combination to a med bowl and mix in the diced bacon, then blend until spread uniformly. Sprinkle with salt & pepper.

7. Top with cauliflower in the ready casserole bowl & crumble over the leftover chèvre.

8. Bake for about twenty mins before the top only starts to shine. Decorate it then with green onions & serve.

Cauliflower Cheesy Alla Vodka Casserole

(Ready in about 50 mins :| Serving 1 | Difficulty: Easy)

Per serving: kcal 214, Fat:14g, Net Carbs:6g Protein:12g

Ingredients

- Well-drained cooked cauliflower florets 8 cups

- Vodka sauce 2 cups

- Whipping cream heavy 2 tbsp

- Butter melted 2 tbsp

- Parmesan cheese 1/3 cup

- Kosher salt 1/2 tsp

- Ground pepper black ¼ tsp

- Provolone cheese 6 slices

- Chopped fresh basil 1/4 cup

Instructions

1. In a big bowl, mix the cauliflower, vodka sauce, strong whipping cream, sugar, Parmesan cheese, flake salt, & black pepper, then mix well.
2. Move to a 9 * 13 Casserole & fill with pieces of Provolone/mozzarella cheese.
3. Bake for 30 to 40 minutes in a hot oven 373 degrees (F) or when the baking dish is simmering & the cheese is melted fully.
4. Take it from the oven and leave for around 10 minutes.
5. Now top it with sliced new basil.

Feta Stuffing and Low-Carb Pumpkin Bread

(Ready in about 45 mins :| Serving 10 | Difficulty: Easy)

Per serving: Cal 288, Fat:25g, Net Carbs:3.5g Protein:11g

Ingredients

- Pumpkin bread cubed 4 cups

- Sage flavored pork sausage roll 16 oz

- Chopped onion 1/2 cup

- Chicken 1/3 cup

- Butter 2 tbsp

- Seasoning bell 1 tsp

- Feta cheese crumbled 3/4 cup

- Chopped fresh parsley 2 tbsp

Instructions

1. Toast cubes of pumpkin bread in a preheated oven of 350 degrees (F) for 8 to 10 mins or until its color changes to a golden brown.

2. Fry both sausage & onions together in a med sauté pan until the onions are tender, and the sausage is completely fried.

3. Squeeze 1/4 of a liquid out of a saucepan.

4. Apply the butter, broth & seasoning of Bell, then carry it to boil.

5. Remove it from fire and whisk gently in the cubes of bread, feta & parsley.

6. Move to the baking dish & bake for twenty mins at 375 ° (F) or when the surface becomes golden brown & mildly crunchy.

7. Bake it for 1 hour & serve hot.

Keto Spicy Sausage and Cheddar Stuffing

(Ready in about 3hour 20 mins :| Serving 16 | Difficulty: Easy)

Per serving: Kcal 311, Fat:26.4g, Net Carbs:6g Protein:11.5g

Ingredients

- Cheesy skillet bread 1

- Italian sausage spicy 12 ounces

- Diced celery 1 cup

- Diced onion 1/2 cup

- Minced garlic cloves 2

- Dried sage 1 tsp

- Kosher salt 1/2 tsp

- Black pepper 1/4 tsp

187

- Chicken broth low sodium 1/2 cup

- large eggs 2

- heavy cream 1/4 cup

Instructions

1. Create the skillet bread & cut into 1/2-inch bits, one day/two in advance. The oven preheated to the 200F.

2. Place the cubes of bread over a wide baking sheet and bake for two to three hrs., until it's dried and crisp. Let them hang out overnight to carry on drying.

3. Heat a large pan on med heat & include sausage; sauté with a wooden spoon only until cooked through, around six mins, breaking up big pieces.

4. Move sausage to the wide bowl, using a spoon with a slot. Apply celery, onion, garlic, basil, salt &

pepper to pan, then sauté for around five mins, until tender. Decorate with bacon.

5. Oven Preheat to 350F, and a big glass. Casserole measuring 13 x 9 inch with butter. Substitute sausage combination of cubed crust. Add the broth and mix the chicken to blend.

6. Stir eggs with milk in a med dish, then spill the mixture into a bowl. Toss and move it to ready Casserole until well mixed. Bake uncovered for 35 mins until the surface is browned & crusty.

Gluten-Free Stuffing & Low-Carb

(Ready in about 18 mins |Serving 1 | Difficulty: Easy)

Per serving: Cal 203, Fat:16g, Net Carbs:4g Protein:8g

Ingredients

- Mild sausage rolls 12 oz

- Chopped onion 1/2 cup

- Chopped celery 1 cup

- Chopped cauliflower1 head

- White wine 1/2 cup

- Chopped walnuts 1/4 cup

- Chopped parsley 1/4 cup

- Minced fresh sage 1 tsp

- Pepper & salt to taste

Instructions

1. Fry your sausage in such a big sauté skillet & cut it into tiny bits. Apply your onions & celery to a saucepan and simmer for 5 mins or until softened.

2. Apply the cauliflower & simmer for about eight minutes. You want to keep it a little darker & caramelize, so don't mix very much. Apply the white wine & boil over med heat until there is no liquid left only at the bottom of a skillet.

3. Add on the walnuts & then fry for 2 minutes. Remove it from fire, and whisk in the sage and parsley. Season it with salt & pepper.

Low-Carb Tortillas

(Ready in about 20 mins |Serving 16 | Difficulty: Easy)

Per serving: Kcal 50, Fat:1.5g, Net Carbs:2.75g
Protein:8.5g

Ingredients

- Large Eggs 8

- Coconut flour 1/3 cup

- Water 10 tbsp

- Baking powder 1/4 tsp

- Garlic powder 1/4 tsp

- Onion Powder 1/4 tsp

- Chili powder 1/4 tsp

- Pink Salt 1/4 tsp

Instructions

1. In a cup, apply the egg, coconut powder, baking soda & water. Mix well (the combination must be standardized and watery).

2. Warm the skillet on lower heat. Wait until the skillet is heated, spray with a baking spray & fall a few of the combination into the middle.

3. Tilt the pan on both corners asap and scatter your batter as evenly as possible.

4. Cook it before it begins to rise or bubble for a few minutes until you pick it up & the different side had browned. Turn & cook for one minute.

5. Repeat until the batter is all fried. For us, the mixture above rendered 16 little taco-sized tortillas.

6. TIP: If the first tortilla might not lay evenly enough on the pan, apply additional water to the white egg mixture and blend it.

Two Mins Low-Carb English Muffin

(Ready in about 4 mins |Serving 2 | Difficulty: Easy)

Per serving: Kcal 222, Fat:20g, Net Carbs:3g Protein:7g

Ingredients

- Unsweetened almond butter cashew 2 tbsp

- Butter 1 tbsp

- Almond flour 2 tbsp

- Salt 1/8 tsp

- Baking powder 1/2 tsp

- Almond milk unsweetened 1 tbsp

- The egg has beaten 1

Instructions

1. Sprinkle with olive oil baking spray/coconut oil spray your ramekin.
2. Apply butter & almond butter to the platter.
3. For thirty-sec microwave, then blend it until smooth. Put aside to chill.
4. Whisk together almond meal/flour, cinnamon, & baking soda/powder in a tiny bowl.
5. To dry products, add the milk & the egg and mix until combined.
6. Place this mixture over almond butter combination into a small ramekin and whisk to mix properly.
7. Microwave it for two mins.
8. Let chill it for a few mins before extracting it from the ramekin & cutting in half toast.
9. Toast if you like.

Cheesy Garlic Bread Muffins

(Ready in about 45 mins |Serving 12 | Difficulty: Easy)

Per serving: Kcal 322, Fat:27.17g, Net Carbs:7.44g
Protein:12.83g

Ingredients

- Melted butter 6 tbsp

- Garlic pressed 5 cloves

- Sour cream 1/2 cup

- Large eggs 4

- Salt 1 tsp

- Almond flour 3 cups

- Baking powder 2 tsp

- Cheddar cheese shredded 1 cup

- Chopped parsley 1/4 cup

- Shredded mozzarella 4 ounces

- Salt for taste

Instructions

1. Oven preheated to 325F, and well grease a regular nonstick muffin pan. Place muffin pan on the wide-rimmed cookie sheet.
2. Mix softened butter & garlic cloves 3.
3. Mix your sour cream, eggs, leftover garlic, & salt in a high-speed blender/food processor. Mixed phase as well. Apply the almond flour/meal, baking powder, bacon, & parsley then begin to cook until smooth.
4. Split halves of batter b/w the ready muffin cups& create a tiny well in the middle of each using a spoon.
5. Split the sliced mozzarella b/w the muffins and push into wells. Sprinkle with such a combination of about 1 teaspoon of garlic butter.
6. Split the leftover batter b/w each cup of muffins, making sure the cheese is coated in the best way

possible. Blend the leftover garlic butter over the tops & sprinkle it with salt.

7. Bake for around 25 mins, until the tops become golden brown as well as solid if touch. They can leak a lot of oil when they bake, and it will leak some over the sides (hence the cookie sheet lower-to save the oven).

8. Remove and allow it to cool for ten mins before serving it to guests. From the oven, they're great and mild only with cheese already gooey. They're cold and heat up quickly too.

Braided Garlic Breadsticks

(Ready in about 35 mins |Serving 8 | Difficulty: Easy)

Per serving: Kcal 229, Fat:18g, Net Carbs:7g Protein:10g

Ingredients

Dough Ingredients:

- Shredded mozzarella 8 oz

- Cream cheese 2 oz

- Egg 1

- Coconut flour 1/3 cup

- Almond flour 1/3 cup

- Golden ground flaxseed 1/3 cup

- Baking powder 2 tsp

Garlic Butter Topping:

- Melted butter 2 tbsp

- Garlic crushed 2 cloves

- Pinch of "salt."

Instructions

1. Oven preheated to 400. Mix both butter & garlic, which is minced. Set Down. Line the baking sheet with parchment.

2. Place cheese in a safe bowl in a microwave oven. 1 min Microwave. Shake. Again, Microwave for thirty sec. Shake. Any cheese will be melting on that stage. Microwave another 30 seconds before uniform & gloopy. Add the ingredients into the egg & dry. You may need to pour it on wax paper, then knead this by hand to mix your ingredients completely, or you may do this with the dough tool of a mixing bowl.

3. Push the bakery release paper into a wide rectangle. Split into 8 lines in a lengthwise direction. Break every strip into three smaller pieces, lengthwise. You're going to end up having twenty-four strips. Apply three strips to roofs. Braid your dough. Connect bottom & tuck under.

Place your braid on the cookie sheet coated with a parchment. Allow producing 8 sticks of braided bread.

4. Clean each of them with garlic butter You need to have some of the small garlic bits on them too. Toss a tiny quantity of salt though on your breadsticks.

5. Cook fifteen Mins to prepare. Remove from heat & coat with the remaining garlic butter. Bake 5 to 10 mins, or its color changes to a golden brown. Serve hot.12. Asiago Zucchini.

Bread and dried Sun Tomato – Low-Carb

(Ready in about 1hour 30 mins |Serving 12| Difficulty: Easy)

Per serving: kcal 262, Fat:23g, Net Carbs:3g Protein:8g

Ingredients

- Salted melted butter 3/4 cup

- Eggs 4

- Almond milk unsweetened 1/2 cup

- Zucchini shredded 1/2 cup, crushed dry in a paper towel

- Dried sun tomatoes chopped 2 tbsp

- Almond flour 2 cups

- Coconut flour 1/4 cup

- Baking powder 4 tsp

- Granulated sugar 1 tsp

- Xanthan gum 1/2 tsp

- Kosher salt 1 1/4 tsp

- Dried oregano 1/2 tsp

- Dried parsley 1/2 tsp

- Garlic powder 1/4 tsp

- Ground asiago cheese 1/2 cup

Instructions

1. Oven Preheated to 350 ° C (F)
2. In a grinder, mix (wet ingredients) together with all the butter, peas, almond milk, zucchini & dried tomatoes, then blend for around thirty seconds or almost smooth.
3. Blend all the (dry ingredients) coconut flour, almond flour, baking soda, sweetener, xanthan gum, cinnamon, oregano, parsley, garlic powder in the med sized bowl and combine with a fork until well mixed without lumps.

4. place the dry ingredients into the wet ingredients and combine with a fork until it creates a smooth batter and absorbs the dry ingredients.
5. Mix in cheese made in Asiago.
6. In a greased loaf tin/twelve muffin cups, spoon your batter.
7. Bake for 1 hr. at 350 ° (F) while creating a loaf.
8. When creating muffins, bake at 350 ° (F) for twenty to twenty-five mins.

Low-Carb Cranberry Relish (Keto)

(Ready in about 15 mins |Serving 12| Difficulty: Easy)

Per serving: Kcal 17, Fat:24g, Net Carbs:4g

Ingredients

- Ocean fresh Spray cranberries 12 ounces

- 4 oz orange 1 med

- Swerve Granulated 2/3 cup

- Fresh ginger juice 1 tsp

- Ground cloves 3 pinches

Instructions

1. Clean your cranberries & remove any weak berries or tiny stones. Slice the stem & the end of Florida State Flower to the skin, then segment it & break in half per slice. Don't take off the orange. Throw out the seeds. Chop a slice of ginger approximately

1 inch. In a coffee/spice grinder, pulverize the sweetener.

2. In the blender lie both cranberries as well as orange bits and apply the sweetener, cinnamon & juice of ginger.

3. In the food processor, blend both the cranberries & orange until they are chopped into approximately the same sized bits. If you like it to be sweeter, apply your preferred stevia sweetener/more crushed Sukrin

4. Refrigerate for up to 2 days until use, usually for 5-7 days. Makes about three cups each serving, plus 1/4 cup.

Parmesan Garlic Roasted Mushrooms

(Ready in about 30 mins |Serving 8| Difficulty: Easy)

Per serving: Cal 151, Fat:14g, Net Carbs:5g Protein:2g

Ingredients

- Cleaned & trimmed mushrooms 1 pound

- Chopped large cloves garlic 3

- Olive oil 2 tbsp

- Minced olives 2 tbsp

- Fresh lemon juice 2 tsp

- Chopped flat-leaf 1/4 c

- Pepper & salt to taste

- Butter 3 tbsp

- Shredded parmesan cheese 1/4 c fresh

Instructions

1. Oven Preheated to 450 degrees and gently spray nonstick oil on a small baking dish. Toss with mushrooms, oil, garlic, olives and capers, lemon juice, salt, parsley, & pepper together in your bowl. Dot the butter uniformly on the upper edge of mushrooms, then roast through the baking process for twenty mins, turning halfway.

2. Take it from your oven, turn that broiler on and cover the oven shelf. Toss the cheese over mushrooms, then move to the oven on top broil & rack before the cheese is melted and start browning for around 3 mins.

Creamy Cauliflower Mash with Kale (Low-Carb Colcannon)

(Ready in about 30 mins |Serving 4| Difficulty: Easy)

Per serving: Kcal 112, Fat:5g, Net Carbs:16g Protein:6g

Ingredients

- One large head cauliflower (6 cups) trim up in florets

- Unsalted butter 4 tsp

- Chopped kale 3 cups

- Crushed garlic 4 cloves

- Minced scallions 2

- Free fat milk 1/3 cup

- Pepper & kosher salt

Instructions

1. Simmer the cauliflower: Place the cauliflower in such a med pot and cover one inch with cold water. Apply salt, then bring it to a boil.
2. Cook, tender before the fork. Six to eight mins. Drain it through a colander (reserve any liquid if necessary).
3. Melt 1 tsp of med-high heat butter in the same pot. Apply the garlic & green onions, fry thirty sec, add the leaf cabbage, 1/4 teaspoon salt, cover & cook until wilted, 6-7 mins.
4. Puree your cauliflower w milk in a processor, move the greens to the pot and apply 1/2 tsp butter, 1/4 tsp salt & pepper.
5. Put it in a bowl and season with leftover tsp butter to eat.

Parmesan Rosti & Low-Carb Celeriac Bacon

(Ready in about 10 mins |Serving 2| Difficulty: Easy)

Per serving: Cal 137, Fat:15g, Net Carbs:4g Protein:5g

Ingredients

- Raw minced bacon, 2 Tbsp

- Butter 1 Tbsp

- Olive oil 2 tsp

- Shredded raw Celeriac 1 cup

- Minced fresh parsley 1 tsp

- Grated Parmesan cheese 2 Tbsp

- Flake salt 1/2 tsp

- Ground black pepper 1/8 tsp

- Garlic powder 1/4 tsp

Instructions

1. Cook your bacon within the olive oil & butter in 12 to 14 inches sauté skillet, until almost all become crispy. In the meanwhile, add and blend well the chopped celeriac, parsley, grated parmesan cheese, salt, pepper & garlic powder. Apply the celeriac combination to the saucepan, then blend well with the fried bacon. Push the mixture onto the hot pan with a broad spoon at the back to create a circular shape.

2. Cook for around five mins at low-med heat, or until its color changes to golden brown (dark) and crispy on the sides & soften the rest. Place the serving platter carefully over the pan and turn the cake crisply side up onto it. Serve warm, decorated with additional parsley If needed.

Garlic Butter Sautéed Spinach

(Ready in about 8 mins |Serving 2| Difficulty: Easy)

Per serving: Cal 71, Fat:4.6g, Net Carbs:4g Protein:3.7g

Ingredients

- Salted melted butter 2 tbsp

- 4 cloves garlic minced

- Baby spinach 8 oz

- Salt 1 pinch

- Lemon juice 1 tsp

Instructions

1. Warm a pan up, then apply the butter. Sauté your garlic until aromatic, apply the spinach to the pan, then incorporate the salt & lemon juice and mix well to blend.
2. Remove from the heat and switch to a serving plate until spinach leaves begin to wilt.
3. Garnish with new slices of lemon and serve right away.

Low-Carb Coconut Creamed Spinach

(Ready in about 4 mins |Serving 1| Difficulty: Easy)

Per serving: Cal 73, Fat:7g, Net Carbs:1g Protein:2g

Ingredients

- Coconut milk 1/4 cup

- Baby spinach 4 cups

- Nutmeg 1/8 tsp

- Granulated sugar 2 tsp

- Cayenne pepper 1/8 tsp

- Salt to taste

Instructions

1. Heat coconut milk for around two mins in a shallow sauté pan. Apply the leaves of spinach and mix until wilted, bright green. Add seasonings, try & adjust when appropriate.
2. Serve it.

Buttery Bacon Brussels Sprouts

(Ready in about 20 mins |Serving 5| Difficulty: Easy)

Per serving: Kcal 120, Fat:10g, Net Carbs:3.8g Protein:3g

Ingredients

- Brussels sprouts 400 g

- Bacon 2 slices

- Butter 55 g

- Crushed garlic 1/2 clove

- Walnuts 4 pieces

Instructions

1. Prepare the sprouts in Brussels by eliminating every dirty leaf, slightly trim the root, and split in half.

2. Simmer in a limited volume of water, about 5 to 8 mins until fully done. Drain and keep the lid off to make the steam run. You wouldn't want a soggy sauce.

3. Heat the butter in a pan and fry the bacon softly before it starts to go crispy. Now apply the garlic and proceed to fry for one minute. Be alert not to make the garlic burnt.

4. Then apply the zest of orange and whisk gently in the sprouts cooked in Brussels. Mix in the buttery garlic sauce when heating the Brussels sprouts to coat them.

5. Serve & use a few bits of walnut for garnish.

Stir-Fried Bok Choy with Soy Butter & Sauce

(Ready in about 15 mins |Serving 4| Difficulty: Easy)

Per serving: Cal 119, Fat:11g, Net Carbs:4g Protein:3g

Ingredients

- Water 2 t

- soy sauce 2 tsp

- sesame oil 1 tsp

- oyster sauce 1 t

- vegetable oil 1 t

- trimmed heads bok choy 2 & cut crosswise in strips

- salt 1/2 tsp

- butter 1 t

Instructions

1. Mix all the water, soy sauce, sesame seed, as well as the oyster sauce.

2. Though until hot, around 1 to 2 mins, heat wok/frying pan, Now add oil & cook for around thirty sec.

3. Apply salt, then bok choy, & stir-fry for two minutes.

4. Apply a combination of soy sauce & butter, then fry for another 1 to 2 mins until bok choy is somewhat crispy but becomes soft.

5. Serve warm, if needed, seasoned with sesame oil.

Low-Carb Cheesy Brussels Sprouts Gratin

(Ready in about 40 mins |Serving 8| Difficulty: Easy)

Per serving: Kcal 253, Fat:19g, Net Carbs:10g Protein:8g

Ingredients

- Removed Brussels Sprouts stems 2 pounds

- Additional virgin olive oil 2 tbsp

- Salt 1/2 tsp

- Pepper 1/4 tsp

- Heavy cream 1 cup

- White cheddar grated 1 cup

- Zest 1 lemon

- White pepper 1/4 tsp

- Asiago cheese grated 1/3 cup

Instructions

1. Oven Preheated to 400 F.
2. Cut Brussels Sprinkles in two, & mix in a bowl of oil.
3. Season with pepper & salt on a baking tray/cast iron pan.
4. Cook for about twenty mins.
5. Mix heavy whipping cream, cheddar, zest of lemon & pepper together in another dish.
6. Place on the Sprouts in Brussels.
7. Sprinkle over dried Asiago.
8. Cook 10 to 15 mins either hot before it bubbles & steams.
9. If needed, season with parsley (fresh).

Low-Carb Creamy Greek Zucchini Patties

(Ready in about 40 mins |Serving 24| Difficulty: Easy)

Per serving: Cal 53, Fat:5g, Net Carbs:2g Protein:2g

Ingredients

- Zucchini 2 lbs.
- Large organic eggs 2
- Fresh herbs large handfuls 2
- Breadcrumbs 1 cup
- Crumbled feta cheese 1 cup
- Ground cumin 1 tsp
- Fine-grain sea salt 1 tsp
- Ground black pepper
- Olive oil 3 tbsp

Instructions

1. Clean the courgettes, then break its end off. Grate these on grates side gaps.

2. In a colander, put grated courgettes, & season with salt. Let drain for a minimum of ten mins (best 1 hour).

3. Take the courgettes handfuls, then suck out all the moisture. Beat the eggs in a big bowl, add the grated courgettes, basil, cumin, almond meal/flour/, feta, pepper & salt. Okay, blend as properly.

4. Move the mixture to the fridge for 20 mins so that the almond meal will soak up more of the moisture.

5. Take a couple of handfuls of combinations & form them into patties. If it is sticky, apply one tbsp of even more almond meal/flour at a time.

6. Heat a tbsp of olive oil on med-high heat in the big nonstick skillet. When the patties are hot cooked in lots (do not overload them) for around five mins each side, until golden brown.

7. Remove and rinse quickly to catch up with the extra oil on a paper towel.

Spaghetti Squash with Garlic and Parsley

(Ready in about 1hour |Serving 4| Difficulty: Easy)

Per serving: Kcal 89, Fat:6g, Net Carbs:8g Protein:3g

Ingredients

- Spaghetti squash 1 large

- Butter soft 3 tbsp

- Chopped small garlic 2 cloves

- Chopped parsley 2-3 tbsp

- Grated parmesan cheese 1/2 cup

- Pepper & salt to taste

Instructions

1. Oven preheated to 375 & put the rack halfway through. Line a baking pan with bakery release paper.

2. Slice the vegetable spaghetti in half-length and pinch the seeds out. Chop the parsley as well as garlic & put in a tiny bowl. Apply the butter melted, then stir it with a spoon.

3. Rub the butter into the cavity and around the sliced parts of the vegetable spaghetti.

4. Cook for 45 to 60 mins.

5. Let it cool so the squash can be treated and scraped off the surface. In Parmesan cheese, salt & pepper to try and blend.

6. Around 3/4 tassels each meal.

Spaghetti Squash with Garlic, Bacon & Parmesan

(Ready in about 50 mins |Serving 6| Difficulty: Easy)

Per serving: Kcal 113, Fat:6g, Net Carbs:11g Protein:2g

Ingredients

- 4 pounds spaghetti squash 1

- Bacon diced 4 slices

- Chopped garlic 3 cloves

- Parmesan cheese shaved

- Pepper & salt

Instructions

1. Oven preheated to 375 °. Spray the cookie sheet with baking spray.

2. Clean the vegetable spaghetti, then pick the stem off the top. Keep this up with side cut down smooth. Cut the squash lengthwise in two.
3. Scrounge the seeds off the squash center and remove. Sprinkle pepper & salt into the squash.
4. Put it on the ready pan and cook for 30 to 45 mins or with just a little resistance, until a fine knife could be quickly placed.
5. Cook the bacon until crispy, on med heat. Apply the garlic to bacon & bake for 1 min, until it is fragrant.
6. Using a fork to remove lengthy strips of flesh from in the squash. Put it in a bowl.
7. Apply bacon & garlic to the squash bowl.
8. Season with salt & pepper, then brush on certain Parmesan cheese.

KETOGENIC DIET

SNACKS COOKBOOK

SNACKS

Graham Crackers Homemade

(Ready in about 20 mins| serving 10 | Difficulty: easy)

Per serving: kcal 156, Fat: 13.3g, net carbs:6.2g, Protein:5.21g

Ingredients

- Almond flour 2 cups
- Swerve brown 1/3 cup
- Cinnamon es2 tsp
- Baking powder 1 tsp
- Pinch salt
- Large egg 1
- Butter melted 2 tbsp
- Vanilla extract 1 tsp

Instructions

1. The oven preheated to 300f for crackers.

2. Whisk the almond/coconut flour, sweetener, spice, baking powder/soda & salt together in a big dish. Add the sugar, softened butter, black treacle & vanilla extract before the dough is combined.

3. Place the dough onto a wide sheet of bakery release paper or filler it with silicone, then pat it into a harsh rectangle. Cover it with such A single sheet of paper. Roll the dough as thinly if possible, To a thickness of around 1/8-1/4 inches.

4. Take Off The top parchment & use the knife or even a pizza Cutter to grade approximately 2 × 2 inches into squares. Place the whole parchment on a cookie sheet.

5. Bake for 20-30 mins, till it becomes brown & strong. Remove crackers, let them cool for 30 Mins, then break down together with score points. Go to a warm oven. Let mix it for the other 30 mins then allow It to cool fully (they crisp up while they cool).

Keto Cinnamon Roll Biscotti

(Ready in about 1hour 20 mins| serving 15 biscotti | Difficulty: medium)

Per serving: kcal 133, Fat: 12g, Net carbs:4g, Protein:5.21g

Ingredients

Filling/topping:

- Swerve sweetener 2 tbsp
- Ground cinnamon 1 tsp

Biscotti:

- Almond flour Honeyville 2 cups
- Swerve sweetener 1/3 cup
- Baking powder 1 tsp
- Xanthan gum 1/2 tsp
- Salt 1/4 tsp

- Melted butter+1 tbsp brushing biscotti 1/4 cup

- Large egg 1

- Vanilla extract 1 tsp

Glaze:

- Powdered Swerve sweetener 1/4 cup

- Heavy cream 2 tbsp

- Vanilla 1/2 tsp

Instructions

1. Mix sweetener & spice into A tiny bowl for filling. Place On aside.

2. Oven preheated to 325f, & line A bakery release paper baking sheet.

3. Whisk the almond/coconut flour, sweetener, baking soda/powder, Xanthan gum & salt together in the bowl. Mix the flour, egg & vanilla 1/4 Cup extract before the dough gets around.

4. Turn the dough on a cookie sheet and split it in two. The form could half into the ten by a four-inch rectangle. Ensure the size & form of both parts are comparable.

5. Sprinkle around 2/3 of cinnamon filling in one part. Place its other half of the dough on top and close that seams & smooth the surface.

6. Bake for 25 mins or until mildly Browned, then only tap solid. Remove the remaining melted butter from the oven and sweep, then dust it with the remaining cinnamon combination. Let it cool for 30 mins, And-the oven to cool down to 250f.

7. Slice logs into around 15 pieces using the fine knife

8. Put slices back on a cookie sheet and bake it for 15 Min, then turn over and bake it for another 15 min. Turn the oven off & Let stay away until it's cold.

9. For the glaze, mix powdered sweetener along with vanilla & cream extract until smooth. Drizzle on Chilled biscotti.

Strawberry Cheesecake Popsicles – Low-Carb and Gluten-Free

(Ready in about 4hour 15 mins| serving 12 popsicles | Difficulty: hard)

Per serving: kcal 122, Fat: 12g, Net carbs:3g, Protein:2g

Ingredients

- Softened cream cheese 8 oz
- Cream 1 cup
- Powdered Swerve sweetener 1/3 cup
- Stevia extract 1/4 tsp
- Lemon juice 1 tbsp
- Lemon zest 2 tsp
- Chopped fresh strawberries 2 cups

Instructions

1. Place and heat your "cream-cheese" In the mixing bowl until smooth.

2. Add milk powder swerve, lime Juice, stevia extract & lemon zest. Mixed phase till well.

3. Attach 1 1/2 cups of raspberries & finish processing until completely smooth. Delete Sliced leftover raspberries.

4. Pour the mixture into molds of popsicle & push Sticks of popsicle around two/three of the way in each.

5. Freeze it for 4 hrs. Run for 20-30 seconds under warm water to unmold, after which turn stick nicely to release.

Keto Cheese Pops – Low-Carb Popcorn

(Ready in about 8 mins :| Serving 1 | Difficulty: easy)

Per serving: kcal 88, Fat:7g, Net carbs:4g Protein:5g

Ingredients

- Hard cheese 100g

Instructions

1. Slice hard cheese into pieces first, and then into little squares.

2. Place it on a cookie sheet with a bakery release paper cover with the napkin.

3. Hold it on 48 hours in the kitchen.

4. Heat the oven until 200 c (392f)

5. Place the cheese inside the oven for three mins.

6. Enjoy your meal.

Dark Chocolate-Covered Walnuts

(Ready in about 30 mins| Serving 2 | Difficulty: easy)

Per serving kcal 160 Total Fat: 13g Net carbs:4.4g, Protein: 3g

Ingredients

- Shelled walnuts 2 cups
- Chocolate chopped unsweetened 4 oz
- Powdered Swerve sweetener ¼ cup
- Walnut oil 3 tbsp
- Vanilla extract ½ tsp
- Cocoa powder unsweetened 1 tbsp

Instructions

1. Line a cookie sheet with bakery release paper.
2. Combine the sugar, swerve powdered & almond oil/walnut Oil on low heat. Mix it until smooth & melted.

3. Whisk in the vanilla extract & Cocoa powder until smooth.

4. To thicken, let Cool for 5 mins.

5. Attach half of the walnuts & raise every walnut out from A fork, tap lightly on the surface to extract excessive coat.

6. Place every walnut mostly on the Ready cookie sheet. Repeat for Leftover walnuts.

7. Place the baking sheet 15-20 mins in the refrigerator.

8. If the coating begins thickening too much, gently Reheat to a little more liquid over low heat.

9. Work for a few walnuts at such a time, re-coating by falling again into the coating of chocolate and pulling out with a pick, pressing to extract any on foot.

10. Put on a cookie sheet, and chill Until solid in the fridge.

Mexican Hot Chocolate – Low-Carb and Gluten-Free

(Ready in about 10mins| Serving 20| Difficulty: very easy)

Per serving kcal 330, Total Fat: 31g Net carbs:3.8g, Protein: 7g

Ingredients

- Almond milk 1 ¼ cup
- Heavy cream ½ cup
- Cocoa powder gluten-free unsweetened 2 tbsp
- Swerve sweetener 1 tbsp
- Ground cinnamon ¼ tsp
- Chipotle powder 1/8-¼ tsp
- Whipped dollop cream & cinnamon sprinkle for garnish

Instructions

1. Mix almond milk, salt, chocolate powder, swerve, spice & chipotle powder into a med saucepan on normal heat.

2. Whisk together as good, after Which carries i t to the simmer.

3. Remove it from fire, divide it B/w 2 mugs, & top it with cinnamon & chantilly cream.

4. Only apply a shot of good Coffee or espresso f or an additional boost.

Homemade Thin Mints (Low-Carb and Gluten-Free)

(Ready in about 1hour| Serving 20 | Difficulty: easy)

Per serving: kcal 116, Fat: 10.4g, Net carbs:7g, Protein: 3g

Ingredients

Cookies:

- Almond Flour 1 3/4 cups
- Cocoa powder 1/3 cup
- Swerve sweetener 1/3 cup
- Baking powder 1 tsp
- Salt 1/4 tsp
- Slightly beaten large egg 1
- Butter melted 2 tbsp
- Vanilla extract 1/2 tsp

Coating:

- Coconut oil & butter1 tbsp

- Lily's dark chocolate 7 oz

- Peppermint extract 1 tsp

Instructions

Cookies:

1. Oven preheated to 300f, & Line 2 cookie sheets with bakery release paper

2. Combine the almond flour, cocoa sugar, sweetener, baking Soda/powder & salt in a big dish. Put the egg, butter as well as vanilla & stir it well until the dough fits in.

3. Roll out the dough b/w 2 pieces of bakery release Paper to optimal thickness but not more than one/four "wide. Take the parchment top Off and put aside.

4. Cut out dough circles using just a 2 inches diameter biscuit cutter and raise softly. Put biscuits on the

ready cookie sheet. Pick up the dough and re-roll scraps till less can be left to roll out.

5. Bake cookies for 20-30 mins once it's strong to touch (this can differ based on how finely you roll the dough). Remove it and allow it to cool. They'll keep crisping up While they chill off.

Chocolate coating:

1. Put a bowl of metal over a pot of softly boiling water, stopping the bowl from entering the water. In a cup, melt the oil & chocolate, stirring until smooth. Mix in the peppermint Extract and clear from steam.

2. Dip the cookies into Cocoa, transform them over Using two forks and cover the cookie as a whole. Take the cookie out and tap the fork softly, mostly on the bowl's side, to remove the excess chocolate, after which put it on a waxed baking sheet with tape.

3. Refrigerate to Complete state.

Apple Cider Donut Bites

(Ready in about 30 mins| Serving 12 | Difficulty: easy)

Per serving: kcal 164, Fat: 13.7g, Net carbs:4.8g, Protein: 6.5g

Ingredients

Donut bites:

- Almond flour 2 cups
- Swerve sweetener 1/2 cup
- Whey protein powder unflavored 1/4 cup
- Baking powder 2 tsp
- Cinnamon 1/2 tsp
- Salt 1/2 tsp
- Large eggs 2
- Cup water 1/3
- Butter melted 1/4 cup

- Apple cider vinegar 1 1/2 tbsp
- Apple extract 1 1/2 tsp

Coating:

- Swerve sweetener 1/4 cup
- Cinnamon 1 to 2 tsp
- Butter melted 1/4 cup

Instructions

1. Oven Preheated to325f, then grease well a tiny muffin pan (use a standard muffin box with 24 cavities).
2. Mix all the almond meal, sweetener, protein powder, dried powder, spices & salt in the large bowl. Whisk until it's mixed in milk, sugar, butter, cider vinegar & apple extract.
3. Divide the mixture between the wells of the prepared tiny muffin pan. Bake for 15-20 mins, until the cupcakes are hard to touch. Remove &

allow it to cool for 10 mins, then Switch to the wire rack to completely cool.

4. Mix both sweetener & spices in a tiny bowl. Dip a full bite of donut in the softened butter, fully covering it. Then roll the combination into each donut snap.

Low-Carb Almond Bark

(Ready in about 25 mins| Serving 20 | Difficulty: easy)

Per serving: kcal 144, Fat: 14g, Net carbs:5g, Protein: 3g

Ingredients

- Swerve sweetener 1/2 cup

- Water 2 tbsp

- Butter 1 tbsp

- Roasted almonds unsalted 1½ cups

- Sea salt ¼ tsp

- Cocoa butter 4 oz

- Chopped chocolate unsweetened 2.5 oz

- Powdered Swerve sweetener½ cup

- Cocoa powder ¾ cup

- Vanilla extract ½ tsp

- Additional Salt

Instructions

1. Line a big cookie sheet. Combine swerve & water in A med saucepan on med heat, stirring periodically. Put to a simmer, and steam for Around 7-9 mins before the mixture blacken. A combination is going to Smoke mildly, that's usual.

2. Remove the butter from the fire & whisk it. Attach the almonds & mix it to coat easily, then mix it in salt.

3. Place the almonds on the Cookie sheet set, splitting any clumps.

4. Melt the coconut butter & chocolate in A strong saucepan on med heat once smooth.

5. Add sifted erythritol powder, then Mix it in cocoa powder, until smooth.

6. Stir in the vanilla Extract and clear it from heat.

7. Reserve the almonds 1/4 Cup and set back. Stir in the Cocoa, the leftover almonds. Put over the same cookie sheet lined with parchment, Holding the nuts in such a single row.

8. Sprinkle with such an extra Estimated almond & sea salt.

9. Cool it.

Keto Pistachio Truffles

(Ready in about 5 mins| Serving 1 | Difficulty: easy)

Per serving: kcal 121, Fat: 12g, Net carbs:0.5g, Protein: 1g

Ingredients

- Mascarpone cheese & softened 1 cup
- Pure vanilla extract 1/4 tsp
- Erythritol sweetener 3 tbsp
- Chopped pistachios 1/4 cup

Instructions

1. Mix the mascarpone, espresso, and sweetener into a tiny bowl.
2. Mix nicely with such a fork Either spatula, until fully mixed & smooth.
3. Place the pistacia vera on a small plate & roll the truffles onto them until they are coated fully.
4. Cool it for Thirty mins, then serve.
5. Place it in the freezer in an airtight jar for about 1 week.

Keto Peanut Butter Cheesecake Bites

(Ready in about 30 mins| Serving 1 | Difficulty: easy)

Per serving: kcal 233, Fat: 22g, Net carbs:4g, Protein: 4g

Ingredients

- Cream cheese & softened 8 oz
- Powdered erythritol 1/4 cup
- Vanilla extract 1 tsp
- Heavy whipping cream 1/4 cup
- Peanut butter 1/4 cup
- Lily's sugar chocolate 3/4 cup
- Coconut oil 2 tsp

Instructions

255

1. Stir cream cheese, erythritol & Heavy cream until smooth.
2. Mix both peanut butter & vanilla Extract until completely blended, set aside.
3. Stir coconut Oil & melted chocolate.
4. Rub silicone cups with a mixture of chocolate & Put it in a refrigerator for five mins.
5. Repeat the last move & Freeze it for ten mins.
6. Put a few lbs of cheesecake fluff In a mug, then freeze it for fifteen mins.
7. Full cups of chocolate to fill soft cheesecake.
8. Put it in the fridge for about 1 hour.

Fat Bombs

(Ready in about 1hour 5mins| Serving 1 | Difficulty: easy)

Per serving: kcal 153, Fat: 16.6g, Net carbs:1.2g, Protein: 0.2g

Ingredients

- Coconut oil 1/2 cup
- Cacao butter 2 ounces
- Freeze-dried raspberries 1/2 cup
- Powdered erythritol sweetener 1/4 cup

Instructions

1. Top a twelve-cup muffin Tray with the liner material. Or use a muffin pan made of silicone.
2. In a medium saucepan, heat the coconut oil & cacao butter at low temperature until fully melted. Now Remove the heat from the pan.
3. In a mixing bowl, crush the freeze-dried strawberries.
4. Add sweetener &crushed berries to a saucepan. Mix until most of the sweetener dissolves.
5. Split the mixture into muffin cups. The strawberry powder falls to the floor — no problems. Only hold the mixture mixed as you push it into each mold, so there's some strawberry powder on top.
6. Refrigerate for one hr Until it's strong. They can keep over Several weeks in the fridge.

Cheesy Pottery Zucchini (Vegetarian Café)

(Ready in about 50 minutes | Difficulty: easy |Servings 4)

Per serving; kcal 155, 12.9 g Fat; 3.5 g Carbs; 0.8 g fibre; 7.6 g Protein; 0.2 g

Ingredients:

- Non-stick cooking spray
- 2 cups of zucchini,
- 2 tablespoons leeks thinly diced,
- 1/2 teaspoon salt
- Freshly ground black pepper,
- 1/2 teaspoon dried basil to taste
- 1/2 tablespoon of dried oregano
- 1/2 cup Cheddar cheese grated,

- 1/4 cup of heavy cream

- 4 Tablespoons Parmesan cheese,

- 1 tablespoon butter freshly grated,

Instructions:

1. Preheat the oven to 370 degrees F. Grease a saucepan gently. Use a non-stick mist for cooking. Add 1 tablespoon of new Garlic, hazelnuts. Place 1 cup of the slices of zucchini in the dish; add 1 spoonful of leeks; sprinkle Season with oil, basil, pepper, and oregano. Finish Cheddar cheese with 1/4 cup. Echo the layers once again. Whisk the heavy cream in a mixing dish with Parmesan, butter, and Garlic. Break this combination over the layer of zucchini and the layers of Cheese.

2. Position in the preheated furnace and cook to the outside for around 40 to 45 minutes until the edges are beautifully browned. Spray with chopped chives, if required.

Chocolate Chip Cookie Dough Bites

(Ready in about 25 minutes | Serving 24 | Difficulty: easy)

Per serving: kcal 110, Fat: 10g, Net carbs:2g, Protein:2g

Ingredients

Cookie dough bites

- Almond flour 2 cups
- Confectioner's swerve sweetener 1/2 cup
- Salt 1/4 tsp
- Melted butter 6 tbsp
- Vanilla extract 1 tsp
- Chocolate chips sugar-free 1/3 cup

Instructions

1. Oven preheated to 300f & line a 9 X 9 inches pan with bakery release paper.

2. Mix the coconut, peanuts, pecan, & Seeds of sunflowers in the food processor. Heat on high until the combination resembles finely textured crumbs.

3. Shift it to a bowl & Mix in the chocolate morsels, cranberries & salt.

4. Melt butter with yacon or even the Fiber syrup in a med saucepan on low heat. When molten, stir until Smooth in powdered sweetener. Place the Vanilla extract in.

5. In the nut/coconut mixture, Whisk your butter mixture until completely mixed. Push uniformly into the ready Baking pan at the rim. To further press it down & compress it as far as possible, have used the flat-bottomed bottle or measurement cup.

6. Bake for twenty-five min, or until the sides become golden brown. Let it cool down entirely within the pan, after which take them out through parchment. Use a fine knife to Cut these into bars.

Cookie Teapots

1. Mix all the almond meal, the Swerve confectioners, and salt in a big bowl. Mix Softened butter & vanilla extract as well as mix in chocolate morsels.

2. Scoop the dough out through curved tbsp & press a couple of times into your palm to help keep it together, then shape it into a ball. Put on a baking sheet lined with Waxed paper & repeat it with leftover dough.

3. If you want, you should stop here Because these are fine as they are. But placing the baking sheet in the refrigerator for one hour.

Keto Cinnamon Butter Cookies Recipe

(Ready in about 30mins| Serving 1 | Difficulty: easy)

Per serving: kcal 146, Fat: 14g, Net carbs:1g, Protein:4g

Ingredients

- Almond meal 2 cups

- Salted butter 1/2 cup

- Egg 1

- Vanilla extract 1 tsp

- Ground cinnamon 1 tsp

- Liquid stevia 1 tsp

Instructions

1. The oven preheated about 300F.

2. In the mixing bowl, stir all the components, an
   d blend until just mixed.

3. Roll in fifteen balls & put on a tray of a
   greased baking sheet.

4. Put in the microwave, bake it for five mins.

5. Cut the
   dough with such a fork and push it hard.

6. Move to oven & cook for 18-20 mins.

7. Let cool it for five mins.

Dark Chocolate Fudgsicles

(Ready in about 8hours 25 mins| Serving 6 | Difficulty: medium)

Per serving: kcal 133, Fat: 14g, Net carbs:3g, Protein:1g

Ingredients

• Coconut milk 13.5 oz

• Cocoa powder 1/4 cup

• Erythritol 1/4 cup

• Stevia glycerite 6 drops

• Xanthan gum rounded 1/8 tsp

Instructions

1. Put everything in a saucepan except stevia & xanthan gum, then brings to a boil. Put Down warmth to maintain it. Make sure that erythritol dissolves & boil to bloom that cocoa powder for fifteen mins.

2. To adjust the flavor of your preference, Apply two drops of stevia glycerite at a time.

3. Put the xanthan gum in your blender & Gently distribute it all over the heated fudgsicle mixture. Stir strongly until It significantly gets thicker. That must be consistent with Chocolate pudding. This is the move stopping a fudgsicles from becoming rock hard in the refrigerator.

4. Cool the blend & Split it into the popsicle mold. Freeze for 8 hrs or longer, and ideally overnight.

Keto Cheese Straws

(Ready in about 50 mins| Serving 48 | Difficulty: easy)

Per serving: kcal 209, Fat: 18.6g, Net carbs:4.5g, Protein:6.3g

Ingredients

- Almond flour 1 ¾ cup

- Coconut flour 2 tbsp

- Salt ¾ tsp

- Xanthan gum ½ tsp

- Garlic powder ½ tsp

- Cayenne optional ¼-½ tsp

- Chopped butter ½ cup

- Sharp cheddar grated 4 ounces

- Egg yolk 1

Instructions

1. Oven preheated to 300f, & line 2 cookie sheet with bake ry release paper.

2. In a food processor, place the almond meal, Coconut fl our, salt, xanthan gum, garlic powder & cayenne. Pulse a couple of times to mix.

3. Sprinkle the butter bits and the grated cheese over. The dry products, then apply the yolk of the egg. Pulse until the dough is fully mixed, then collect it into a ball.

4. Move the dough to an open star tip-fitted Piping bag & pipe your dough into three inches rows. They could be quite tight Together because they're not expanding. (then you can bring your dough to the cookie press & make enjoyable shapes).

5. Bake for 20-25 minutes until golden brown, then stop your oven & let the straws stay inside for another five mins. Keep a keen watch on them, so that they wouldn't get too much brown.

6. Remove from the pan & let it cool fully.

Everything Bagel Cucumber Bites

(Ready in about 25 mins| Serving 8 | Difficulty: medium)

Per serving: kcal 93, Fat: 7.9g, Net carbs: 2.7g, Protein: 1.5g

Ingredients

Everything bagel seasoning:

- Poppy seeds 1 tsp

- Sesame seeds 1 tsp

- Dried minced garlic 1/2 tsp

- Dried minced onion 1/2 tsp

- Crushed caraway seeds 1/4 tsp

- Coarse salt 1/4 tsp

Cucumber bites:

- Medium cucumber 1

- Cream cheese 4 ounces

- Butter softened 2 tbsp

- Greek yogurt 2 tbsp

- Garlic powder 1/2 tsp

- Salt 1/4 tsp

Instructions

Everything bagel seasoning:

1. Whisk all of the ingredients with Each other in a bowl. Place On aside.

Cucumber Snacks:

1. Use a fine knife to Cut off the cucumber. Cross-slice that cucumber into 1/4 "thick Pieces & placed on the platter.

2. Hit the cream cheese, butter, milk, garlic powder & salt in a med bowl until they are well mixed and smooth.
3. Attach a star-shaped tip to the piping bag & Fill the bag with a combination of cream cheese. Decoratively pouring the Cucumber slices on top.
4. Sprinkle with all bagel seasoning on every slice and serve

Homemade Chicharrones

(Ready in about 3hours 50 mins:| Serving 1 | Difficulty: easy)

Per serving: kcal 152, Fat: 9g, Protein:17g

Ingredients

• Pork back fat & skin 3-5 lbs.

• Extra cooking oil

• Sea salt-taste

• Pepper-taste

Instructions

1. Oven preheated to 250f & set A rack of wire over a cookie sheet.

2. Cut pork skin & fat into long strips, around 2 inches wide, using a keen knife. Score the fat every 2 Inches on every stripe. Insert the knife carefully on 1 end of the strip between the skin & fat, then removes a portion of fat.

3. Once that first part of fat has been erased, it can hold the skin in 1 Hand while sliding a knife down the strip to remove most of the fat. Once more, a little bit of fat that still clings to the skin is fine.

4. Cut each stripe into two-inch squares & put, fat-side down, on wire rack whenever the fat has been removed.

5. In the meantime, if you want to cook the chicharrones with the pork fat, place them in the large saucepan on med heat. Cook gently, about 2 hrs, until most of the fat has liquified. This is also the way you could even render lard besides future use in cooking. To remove the remaining Solids, choose a slotted spoon.

6. When the baking time is up, heat oil/lard into the pan to a depth of 1/3. Or you can have just a few other inches of oil & cook the pork rinds in lots. Oil must be hot, but it should not bubble.

7. Add pork rinds & cook it for about 3-5 Mins, until they bubble & puff up. Erase & sink onto a towel-lined sheet of paper. Instantly sprinkle with salt & pepper.

Keto Cheddar Jalapeno Meatballs

(Ready in about 45 mins:| Serving 8 | Difficulty: easy)

Per serving: kcal 368, Fat: 24g, Net carbs:1.1g
Protein:33.4g

Ingredients

• Ground beef 1 ½ lbs.

• Sharp cheddar grated 6 ounces

• Pork rind crumbs ½ cup

• Large egg 1

• Large jalapeno diced

• Chopped cilantro 2 tbsp

• Chili powder 1 tsp

• Garlic powder 1 tsp

- Salt 1 tsp

- Cumin ½ tsp

- Pepper ½ tsp

Instructions

1. Oven preheated to 375 & line the Bakery release paper with a big rimmed cookie sheet.

2. Mix all the ingredients into the A bowl of a big food processor. A process on high until excellently combined, scraping Away from the processor's sides as needed.

3. Alternatively, you can mix everything by hand in a bowl. To form a cohesive mixture, genuinely working the ingredients together.

4. Roll into 1½-inch balls and place on the ready cookie sheet about 1 inch apart. Bake for twenty mins, Till cooked & browned.

5. Serve warm.

Taco Bites (Mini)

(Ready in about 35 mins:| Serving 32 | Difficulty: easy)

Per serving: kcal 329, Fat: 22.15g, Net carbs:3.1g
Protein:25.2g

Ingredients

• Ground beef grass-fed O organics 1 lb.

• O organics melted salted butter 2 tbsp.

• Taco seasoning 3 tbsp

• Large egg 1

• O organics shredded cheese Mexican blend 6 ounces

• Salsa O organics 1 cup

• Other garnish

Instructions

1. In a wide skillet on med heat, the meat is sauteed, separating the Clumps by using the wooden spoon, until nearly cooked through.

Add seasoning to the taco & Proceed to sauté until thoroughly cooked. Take off heat & allow it to cool.

2. To 350F, preheat the oven and spray the butter (melted) with a decent nonstick tiny muffin cup. This recipe produces about thirty-two tiny muffins, so if more than 1 mini muffin tray you don't have, you can need to operate in batches.

3. Beat the eggs into a big bowl. Add taco meat & the Grilled cheese on 4 ounces. Mix it completely.

4. Sprinkle with the leftover melted cheese & muffin cups are filled to around 3/4 complete. Bake for 15-20 mins, until puffed to touch & strong. Remove, and allow to cool for ten mins. Using a small, lightweight spatula to Pass along the side to release muffins.

5. Serve taco toppings include sauce, sour cream & guacamole for your pick.

Stuffed Baby Peppers

(Ready in about 10 mins | Serving 4-6 | Difficulty: easy)

Per serving 28kcal, fat: 2g, protein: 1g

Ingredients

- Baby peppers

- Cream cheese

Instructions

1. Clean every baby pepper and cut the top off, scooping out any little seeds that might exist.

2. Slowly stuff every pepper with cream cheese with a fine knife before they are finished.

3. Place in the refrigerator for up to three days.

Spanakopita Hand Pies

(Ready in about 40 mins:| Serving 16 | Difficulty: easy)

Per serving: kcal 123, Fat: 9.5g, Net carbs:3.4g
Protein:5.6g

Ingredients

• Spinach thawed frozen 6 ounces

• Crumbled feta cheese 1 cup

• Large egg 1

• Chopped onion 1/4 cup

• Garlic minced 1 clove

• Salt 3/4 tsp

• Pepper 1/2 tsp

- Mozzarella dough 1

- Extra almond flour to roll out.

Instructions

1. Oven Preheated to 350F.

2. Put the spinach in a dish towel & force the extra moisture out. Shift to Wide bowl. Add the feta, potato, cabbage, garlic, salt, & pepper, then mix until good.

3. Sprinkle any 2 to 3 tsp of almond flour on a work surface. Roll the dough out to around sixteen inches by sixteen inches in a wide rectangle. Cut it into sixteen equal squares using such a sharp knife or a pizza cutter.

4. Place around one spinach combination tbsp into the middle of each rectangle. Roll the dough square diagonally over to create a pastry formed like a triangle. When the dough splits or

falls as it bends, easily pinch back & shape across the filling.

5. Put the triangles on a prepared cookie sheet & create a small slit only at the top of each to make the steam to exit. Bake until golden brown, For 20 mins. Remove from the skillet & let it cool.

Keto Buffalo Chicken Sausage Balls

(Ready in about 40 mins:| Serving 12 | Difficulty: easy)

Per serving: kcal 255, fat: 14.02g, Net carbs: 3.90g Protein:14.5g

Sausage balls Ingredients

• Chicken sausage 24 ounces

• Cheddar cheese 1 cup shredded

• <u>Almond flour</u> 1 cup

• <u>Coconut flour</u> 3 tbsp

• Sauce buffalo wing 1/2 cup

• Salt 1 tsp

• Pepper ½ tsp

• Cayenne 1/2 tsp

Dipping sauce bleu cheese ranch:

- Mayonnaise cup 1/3

- Almond milk unsweetened 1/3 cup

- Garlic minced 2 cloves

- Dried parsley ½ tsp

- Dried dill 1 tsp

- Pepper ½ tsp

- Salt ½ tsp

- Cheese crumbled bleu ¼ cup

Instructions

Balls Sausage:

1. To 350F, preheat the oven and line 2 wide cookie sheets with bakery release paper.

2. Combine the bacon, cheddar cheese, buffalo sauce, coconut flour, almond flour, cayenne

salt, and pepper in a wide dish. Combine completely.

3. Roll into balls, one inch & put on prepared sheet for baking around an inch apart. Bake for 25 mins until it becomes golden brown.

Dipping sauce:

1. In a medium dish, add mayonnaise, garlic, dill, almond milk, parsley, pepper, and salt. Then stir and blend with cheese crumbled bleu.

Keto Rosemary Parmesan Crackers

(Ready in about 1hour 10 mins:| Serving 10 | Difficulty: easy)

Per serving: kcal 179, Fat: 15.1g, Net carbs:5.6g, Protein:8.5g

Ingredients

- Sunflower seed flour 2 cups

- Finely grated parmesan 3/4 cup

- Fresh rosemary chopped 2 tbsp

- Garlic powder 1/2 tsp

- Baking powder 1/2 tsp

- Salt 1/2 tsp

- Large egg 1

- Melted butter 2 tbsp

- Coarse salt for sprinkling

Instructions

1. Oven Preheated to 300F.

2. Combine the seed flour of sunflower, parmesan, rosemary, ginger, baking powder/soda & salt in a large dish.

3. Mix within butter & egg before the dough falls around.

4. Turn the dough out & pat it into the harsh rectangle onto a broad silicone cookie sheet. Using a large sheet of Bakery release paper on the cover. Stretch out to a thickness of around 1/4-1/8 inches. Put the Parchment aside.

5. To grade into 2-inch pieces, use a fine knife or pizza wheel. Sprinkle the Sea salt. Move to a broadsheet of a cookie sheet.

6. Bake 40-45 mins, or until the sides are golden brown & the crackers are solid if touch. Remove

and let it cool down before breaking up entirely.
They'll keep crisping Up while they cool.

7. The
   recipe generates around 40 crackers, based on
   how finely the dough is rolled.

Low-Carb Pepperoni Pizza Bites

(Ready in about 18 mins:| Serving 24 | Difficulty: easy)

Per serving: kcal 81, Fat: 6g, Net carbs: 1g Protein: 5g

Ingredients

• Pepperoni 24 slices

• Small basil leaves 24

• Pizza sauce small 1 jar

• Mozzarella balls 24 mini

Instructions

1. Oven preheated to 400F. Snip four 1/2-inch cut-outs along the sides of Each pepperoni slice using kitchen shears, leaving the middle uncut. Per pepperoni will appear Like a circular arrow.

2. Push down every pepperoni into a tiny muffin tin. Bake until the sides are crispy for 5-6 Mins; however, the pepperoni is always hot. Let allow the pepperoni chill within pans to crisp for 5 mins, so they retain their form. Then transfer the cups onto a lined sheet of paper towel to extract excess liquid.

3. Wipe the oil with a towel out of the muffin Tray, after which return the cups to the tray. In the bottom of each cup, put a tiny basil leaf, accompanied by 1 Tsp of pizza sauce, a small mozzarella nut, as well as an olive slice.

4. Return to the oven for two-three mins Before the cheese begins to melt. Allow the cups for 3- 5 mins to chill more before serving.

Pickle Rollups

(Ready in about 12 mins:| Serving 4 | Difficulty: easy)

Per serving: kcal 286, Fat: 26g, Net carbs:4g Protein:10g

Ingredients

- Corned beef lunch meat 8 slices

- Softened cream cheese 4 oz

- Dill pickles 4 med

Instructions

1. Place corned beef on a rough surface in the stacks of 2.

2. Place one ounce of cream Cheese over each stack. Put a pickle Right in each middle. Roll the corned beef across the pickles, then split into 4 equal pieces per slice.

Two Ingredient Cheese Crisps

(Ready in about 22 mins:| Serving 1 | Difficulty: easy)

Per serving: kcal 82, Fat: 6g, Net carbs:1g Protein:6g

Ingredients

- Shredded cheese 1 cup

- Egg whites only 2

Instructions

1. Oven Preheated to 400.

2. Mix the white egg, cheddar, & any Herbs/spices into a tiny bowl.

3. Grease a twenty-four slot mini muffin tray into muffin tins & drop very tiny parts of the cheese mixture.

4. Spread it out, making it as thin to keep it crispy.

5. Bake it for 10-20 mins.

6. Let It cool before eating.

Low-Carb Pinwheels with Bacon and Cream Cheese

(Ready in about 15 mins:| Serving 10 | Difficulty: easy)

Per serving: kcal 143, Fat: 12g, Net carbs:2g Protein:6g

Ingredients

• Ham 18 slices

• Bacon cooked 5 to 8 slices

• Cream cheese 4 oz

• Ranch seasoning 1-1/2

• Chopped black olives ¼ cup

Instruction

1. Put the salami/ham down into 4x2 Alternating rows on a cutting board.

295

2. Spread the salami over the cream cheese. If the cream cheese becomes too hard to apply with a knife, you may attempt to arrange It b/w 2 wax paper sheets & roll it out with a rolling pin, then bring it on the salami or ham.

3. Sprinkle the cream cheese on the Ranch seasoni ng, then apply the black olives.

4. Shortly place
your slices of bacon over the cream cheese.

5. Turn the pinwheels slowly long side-long side, spinning as stiffly as possible.

6. Securely keep the roll, then break it into 1-2 "parts.

7. Use as an appetizer, or individually package each portion with a greaseproof paper for single servings.

Keto Soft Pretzel

(Ready in about 29 mins:| Serving 6 | Difficulty: easy)

Per serving: kcal 449, Fat: 35.5g, Net carbs: 10g, Protein:27.8g

Ingredients

- Baking powder 1tbsp

- Garlic powder 1tbsp

- Onion powder 1 tbsp

- Large egg 3

- Shredded mozzarella cheese 3 cups

- Cream cheese 5 tbsp

- Salt for topping

Instructions

1. Oven preheated to 425 °. Line a rimmed cookie sheet with bakery release paper.

2. Add the almond flour/meal, baking powder/soda, garlic powder & onion powder in a med bowl. Blend until it's combined.

3. Smash 1 of the eggs in a tiny bowl & fork whisk. It would be the wash of the egg for the top of the pretzels as well as the other 2 eggs for the dough.

4. Add mozzarella cheese & cream cheese in a big microwave safe blending bowl. Microwave it for One min and 30 sec. Now remove it from the microwave & blend to mix.

5. Apply the remaining two eggs & the mixture of almond flour to the mixing bowl. Combine until all ingredients are fully mixed. If The dough becomes too stringy and impracticable, just place it back in the oven for 30 seconds to loosen & continue to blend.

6. Split the dough into six equal parts. Roll each piece into a large, thin piece that resembles a breadstick. Fold each piece into the form of a pretzel.

7. Rub the egg wash Over the top within each pr etzel.

8. Brush over the surface with coarse sea salt.

9. Bake 12 to 14 Mins on a center rack.

Fathead Sausage Rolls

(Ready in about 45 mins:| Serving 6 | Difficulty: easy)

Per serving: kcal 470, Fat: 39.1g, Net carbs:3.6g
Protein:26g

Ingredients

- Sausages 500 g

- Onion flakes to garnish

Fathead pastry

- Grated mozzarella 170 g

- 85 g almond meal/flour

- Cream cheese 2 tbsp

- Egg 1

- Pinch salt

- Onion flakes 1 tsp

Instructions

Pre-cook the sausages

1. Using
   a fine knife, cut your sausage casing down the mi
   ddle. Peel the wrapping back.

2. Put every sausage on even A lined oven tray
   & cook for ten mins at 180c/350f.

Fat Pastry head

1. Bake the fat head Pastry while frying the sausages.

2. In a microwave cup, put together the
   shredded/grated cheese and the almond flour/meal. Add
   your cream cheese. Now microwave it for one minute.

3. Then pulse over high for a thirty sec. Detach and mix
   Again. Add the flakes of onion, salt & egg.

4. Put your fat head pastry b/w two pieces of Bakery
   release paper & roll into a small, rectangular bowl.

5. Cut your fat head pastry on one side & put the Sausages around the edge. Start rolling it, then cut off the excessive pastry.

6. Slice Into sausage rolls & drizzle/spray the oil over the end. Sprinkle with flakes of onion to garnish.

7. Bake for 12 to 15 minutes at 220c/425f, until it's crispy all over.

Salt and Vinegar Zucchini Chips

(Ready in about 12hours 15 mins:| Serving 8 | Difficulty: easy)

Per serving: kcal 40, Fat: 3.6g, Net carbs: 2.9g Protein: 0.7g

Ingredients

• Thinly sliced zucchini 4 cups

• Additional virgin olive oil 2 tbsp

• White balsamic vinegar 2 tbsp

• Sea salt 2 tsp

Instructions

1. Using an as small as Possible mandolin or a slice of zucchini.

2. Mix the olive oil & Vinegar in a tiny bowl together.

3. In a wide bowl, put the zucchini, and mix it with oil & vinegar.

4. Add
   the zucchini to the dehydrating In even layers & sprinkle it with the coarse salt.

5. The drying period would differ based on how thin you cut the zucchini and the dehydrator, anywhere from 8 to 14 hrs. I set the temperature of 135F.

6. Line the baking sheet with bakery release paper in the oven. Spread the zucchini uniformly. Bake around 200 degrees f for 2 to 3 hrs.

7. The chips are placed inside an airtight jar.

Cheesy Bacon Zucchini Skins

(Ready in about 20 mins:| Serving 12 | Difficulty: easy)

Per serving: kcal 127, Fat: 11g, Net carbs:2g Protein:4g

Ingredients

• Bacon 6 slices

• Zucchini 3 medium

• Monterey jack cheese chopped 1 cup

• Green onions sliced 3

• Sour cream 1 cup

Instruction

1. Chop the bacon & sauté over med heat in a frying pan until crispy, drain it on towels.

2. Break the zucchini lengthwise in two. Split in half and slice off each zucchini's ends, making four skins, comprising twelve skins.

3. Using a wide spoon, scoop tightly out the white portion of the zucchini leaving around 1/4 "within the skins. Remove the interior of the zucchini and put the skins cut side up on a large baking sheet.

4. Scatter with cheese & crumbled bacon uniformly. Bake for 5 to 10 mins at 400 degrees or until the cheese is finished and the zucchini is somewhat soft (they can always have a little crunch).

5. Before topping with green onion, let it chill for 5 mins and serve it with sour cream/ranch dressing to dip.

Bacon Jalapeño Cheese Ball

(Ready in about 2hour 10 mins:| Serving 1 | difficulty: easy)

Per serving: kcal 110, Fat: 9g, Net carbs:2g Protein:4g

Ingredients

• Softened cream cheese 1 8 ounce

• Jalapeño diced chopped 5 tbsp

• Cooked bacon divided ☐ cup

• Garlic salt ¾ tsp

• Liquid smoke ¼ tsp

Instructions

1. Combine milk softened cheese with 3 tsp jalapeno, one/three cup bacon, garlic salt & liquid smoke in a med bowl.

2. Shape into a ball, cover in plastic wrap, and cool down for 2 hours.

3. Now remove the cheese ball from plastic wrap & roll onto the leftover jalapenos & crumbled bacon to cover.

Low-Carb Everything Crackers

(Ready in about 50 mins:| Serving 36 | Difficulty: easy)

Per serving: kcal 212, fat: 17.1, Net carbs:5.8g Protein:8.1g

Ingredients

• Large egg

• Garlic powder 1/2 ts

• Onion Powder 1/2 tsp

• Kosher Salt 1/4 tsp

• Bagel seasoning 2 tbsp

• Fine almond flour 1&3/4 cups

Instructions

1. Oven preheated to 350f. Mix the seasoning bagel's 1 tbsp, egg, garlic powder, onion powder & salt.

2. Add the almond flour and blend until it forms a pastry. Flatten among 2 sheets of bakery release paper or even on a waxed paper and a Silpat. Spread out to a thickness of 1/8.

3. Sprinkle with the waxed paper on the remaining spoonful of bagel seasoning and press into bread.

4. Use a knife or pizza cutter to cut into squares.

5. Directly transfer parchment or Silpat to the baking sheet.

6. Cook 10 minutes. Test to see if brown is cooked in golden color. If not, so put another 2 minutes.

Peanut Butter Granola

(Ready in about 40 mins | serving 12 | Difficulty: easy)

Per serving: kcal 338, fat: 30.08g, net carbs: 9.74g,
Protein: 9.36g

Ingredients

• Almonds 1 1/2 cups

• Pecans 1 1/2 cups

• Almond flour or shredded coconut 1 cup

• Sunflower seeds 1/4 cup

• Swerve sweetener 1/3 cup

• Collagen protein powder or vanilla whey protein powder
1/3 cup

• Peanut butter 1/3 cup

• Butter 1/4 cup

- Water 1/4 cup

Instructions

1. Oven preheated to 300f & line a large baking paper with a covered baking tray.

2. In the mixing bowl, process the almonds and pecans with larger pieces until they resemble-fine scraps. Mix in chopped nuts, sweetener, sunflower seeds & vanilla whey protein and transfer it to the large bowl.

3. Evaporate peanut butter & butter together in a non - stick frying pan.

4. Place melted peanut butter over a mixture of nut and mix excellently, tossing lightly.

5. Mix the mixture. Combination clumps around each other.

6. Spread the mixture evenly over the ready baking sheet & bake for 30 mins, mixing through halfway. Remove, and allow it to cool.

Keto Salted Caramel Hot Chocolate

(Ready in about 6 mins | serving 1 | difficulty: easy)

Per serving: kcal 210, Fat: 16g, net carbs: 4.5g, Protein: 14.4g

Ingredients

- Hemp milk or unsweetened almond 1/2 cup

- Heavy whipping cream 2 tablespoon

- Cocoa powder 1 tbsp

- Salted caramel collagen 1-2 tbsp

- Liquid or powdered sweetener

- (optional) whipped cream lightly sweetened

- (optional) caramel sauce sugar-free

Instructions

1. In a small saucepan over medium heat, combine the almond or hemp milk and the heavy cream. Bring it to a simmer.

2. Add the cocoa powder and collagen to a blender. Pour in the hot milk and blend until frothy. Taste and adjust for sweetness.

3. Top with lightly sweetened whipped cream and some homemade caramel sauce to take it over the top

Keto Brownie Bark

(Ready in about 45 mins | serving 12 | Difficulty: medium)

Per serving: kcal 98, Fat: 8.3g, net carbs: 4.3g, Protein: 2.4g

Ingredients

- Almond flour 1/2 cup
- Baking powder 1/2 tsp
- Salt 1/4 tsp
- Egg whites 2 large
- Swerve sweetener granular 1/2 cup
- Cocoa powder 3 tbsp
- Instant coffee (optional) 1 tsp
- Butter melted 1/4 cup
- Heavy whipping cream 1 tbsp
- Vanilla 1/2 tsp
- Chocolate chips sugar-free 1/3 cups

Instructions

1. Oven preheated to 325f, and line a baking sheet with bakery release paper. Greaseproof paper to the bakery release paper.

2. Stir together all the baking powder, almond powder as well as salt in the small bowl.

3. Beat a white egg in the large mixing bowl until they're frothy. Beat until smooth in cocoa powder, sweetener & instant coffee, after which beat in softened butter, vanilla & cream. Beat in a mixture of almond meal until it's combined.

4. Spread batter over nonstick baking paper in a 12 by 8-inch rectangle. Stir the chocolate morsels.

5. Bake and set for 18 mins, until puffed. Now remove it from the oven and turn off the Oven and allow to cool for 15 mins.

6. To cut it into 2inch squares, use a filet knife or pizza cutter but don't separate. Return it to a hot oven for 8-10 mins to gently crisp up.

7. Remove, allow it cool down & then split it into squares.